St. Thomas, the Apostle, in India

SILVER BUST OF THE APOSTLE THOMAS AT ORTONA IN ITALY.

ST. THOMAS, THE APOSTLE, IN INDIA.

An Investigation based on the latest researches in connection with the Time-honoured Tradition regarding the martyrdom of St. Thomas in Southern India

BY

F. A. D'CRUZ, K.S.G.,

Retired Superintendent, General Records, Government Secretariat, Madras, and Editor, "The Catholic Register," San Thomé.

TOMB OF ST. THOMAS, SAN THOME.

MADRAS:

PRINTED BY HOE AND CO. AT THE "PREMIER" PRESS.

1922.

A. F. W.

Carpentier

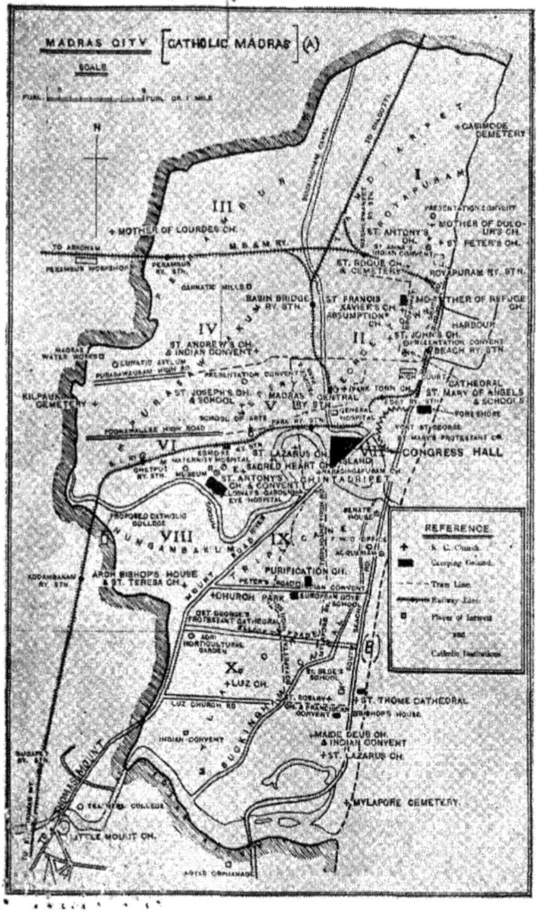

(A) PLAN OF MADRAS CITY AFTER MARIAN CONGRESS MAP.

(B) ROAD DIVIDING MADRAS ARCHDIOCESE FROM MYLAPORE DIOCESE.

CONTENTS.

PAGE

Introduction by Very Rev. Mgr. A. M. Teixeira, Vicar-General and Administrator of the Diocese of San Thomé vii

PART I.

St. Thomas, in the Bible and Tradition.

I. The Bible Record 1
II. The Tradition 3

PART II.

The Discussion.

I. Connection with India 4
II. In Southern India 12
III. Dr. Medlycott on the subject 26
IV. The doubt about the Martyrdom 32
V. The Martyrdom—Different Versions .. 35
VI. The Malabar Tradition 38
VII. The Traditional Record according to Dr. Medlycott 40
VIII. Calamina 42
IX. Mylapore 46
X. Conclusions 50

PART III.

Some Minor Objections.

I. India of the Ancients 52
II. St. Pantænus 54
III. The Jews 57
IV. Ecclesiastical support to the Tradition .. 58

PART IV.

The Legends.

I. Miracles—In Poetry 60
II. The Log 63
III. St. Thomas' Mount 64
IV. The Little Mount 66
V. Concluding Remarks 67

Authorities Consulted 69

LIST OF ILLUSTRATIONS.

SILVER BUST OF THE APOSTLE THOMAS AT ORTONA IN ITALY. *Frontispiece.*

To face page

PLAN OF MADRAS CITY—AFTER MARIAN CONGRESS MAP .. iii

THE PRESENT CATHEDRAL AT SAN THOME vii

THE OLD CATHEDRAL, SAN THOME 1

ST. THOMAS' MOUNT 3

STAINED GLASS, CATHEDRAL, TOURS FRANCE 9

Explanation —First and second bays contain scenes based on the 'Golden Legend' regarding the Apostle Thomas; third and fourth bays have scenes of the life of St Stephen the Martyr.

Left bottom: (1) King Gondophares sends Habban to engage a builder. (2) Christ instructs Thomas to go to India (3) Christ consigns Thomas to Habban. (4) Habban and Thomas embark for India. (5) Banquet feast, King and others present. (6) Thomas is struck on the cheek by the cup-bearer. (7) Cup-bearer killed by a lion. (8) Thomas at the King's request blesses the bride. (9) Thomas before King Gondophares (10) Thomas distributes the King's money in alms. (11) Destruction of the idol (the devil in the form of a black monster). (12) The high priest kills Thomas

COINS OF KING GONDOPHARES 10

STAINED GLASS OVER THE HIGH ALTAR IN THE CATHEDRAL AT SAN THOME 12

INTERIOR OF CATHEDRAL AT SAN THOME 26

SLAB OF CHALCEDONY WHICH COVERED THE APOSTLE'S RELICS AT CHIOS, NOW IN THE CATHEDRAL AT ORTONA, SHOWING FIGURE BUST AND GREEK INSCRIPTION .. 30

ALTAR OF ST. THOMAS, CATHEDRAL, ORTONA, ITALY, UNDER WHICH THE APOSTLE'S RELICS REPOSE .. 31

PORTAL OF THE CHURCH OF "NOTRE DAME," SEMUR, CÔTE D'OR, FRANCE 35

RELIQUARY CONTAINING FRAGMENT OF A BONE AND POINT OF A LANCE IN SAN THOME CATHEDRAL AND REVERSE OF THE RELIQUARY 37

To face page

STAINED GLASS, CATHEDRAL, BOURGES, FRANCE .. 40

Explanation—First Medallion, bottom. right (1) Christ orders Thomas to proceed to India (the gate indicates departure from Caesarea). (2) Thomas presented to the King. (3) Marriage banquet. (4) Cup-bearer attacked by a wild beast.

Second Medallion: (1) Thomas blesses the bride and bridegroom (2) Thomas before a King (Gondophares). (3) King orders the construction of a palace (4) Thomas points to heaven where the palace has been erected.

Third Medallion: Thomas sentenced and sent to prison. (2) Thomas distributes blessed bread, or communion, to his converts. (3) He blesses Mygdonia while in prison. (4) Perhaps an apparition of the Apostle after death.

THE TOMB OF ST. THOMAS IN THE CATHEDRAL AT SAN THOME 46

PLAN OF SAN THOME ABOUT 1635—FROM A DRAWING BY P. B. DE REZENDE PRESERVED IN THE BRITISH MUSEUM. 58

ALTAR OF THE CHURCH ON ST THOMAS' MOUNT .. 60

ANCIENT STONE IMAGE OF ST THOMAS AT MYLAPORE .. 62

ANCIENT PICTURE OF THE BLESSED VIRGIN AT ST. THOMAS' MOUNT PAINTED ON WOOD 64

INTERIOR OF CHURCH ON ST THOMAS' MOUNT 64

ANCIENT CROSS AT ST. THOMAS' MOUNT 65

THE LITTLE MOUNT CHURCH 66

MARBLE ALTAR OF ST. THOMAS IN THE CAVE AT THE LITTLE MOUNT 67

MIRACULOUS SPRING AT THE LITTLE MOUNT 68

THE PRESENT CATHEDRAL AT SAN THOMÉ. CONSECRATED IN 1896.

INTRODUCTION.

The travels, labours, and martyrdom of St. Thomas, the Apostle, have always been a topic of absorbing interest. More literature has perhaps been written on the question of the journeys of the "Unbelieving Apostle" by writers catholic and non-catholic than on any other—St. Peter's excepted. Serious doubts based on so-called "Historic Criticism" have been raised as to the traditional length and breadth of the field covered by the preaching of this Apostle of Christ. Some critics, while they are not disposed to accept the possibility of the Gospel having been preached in the Malabar and the Coromandel Coasts by St. Thomas, deign at least to admit that he preached the Gospel in the extreme north-west of India;—but that he ever crossed over to Southern India—is indeed to them a "hard saying". The coins now in the British Museum and elsewhere of King Gondophernes, or Gondophares, who ruled over those regions at the time of St. Thomas, and the latter's connection with his Court, seem to leave no doubt in the minds of such critics as to the fact that St. Thomas preached the Gospel in his kingdom—that is, in the north-west corner of the Indian Peninsula. As to his having crossed over from the North to Southern India, however, is questioned by them, since, as they allege, they can see no evidence forthcoming. They have therefore tried to relegate the existing tradition in the South to the Limbo of legend, or—of a "*quid pro quo*."

Now, the author of the present work, Mr. F. A. D'Cruz, K.S.G., while he does not hesitate to bring forward, as far as possible, all the objections that have been raised against the time-honoured tradition, has, on the other hand, very ably gathered together in a nutshell all that can be said in support of the tradition that St. Thomas preached and suffered martyrdom in Southern India—drawing his arguments from the *data* supplied both by writers sceptic and by writers believing. He has left out of consideration every statement and shade of opinion which might be called in question. He gives us in this work the cream of the evidence thus far unquestioned—gleaned with great patience from a deep comparative study of different authors on the subject—and which may with confidence be said at least to support very strongly the tradition of the apostolate and martyrdom of St. Thomas in Southern India.

The author's position is (1)—that, even if the evidence so far available is not such as to compel belief, it nevertheless argues very strongly in favour of the tradition which places the martyrdom of St. Thomas in Southern India; and (2)—that the writers who have tried to discredit, or disprove, it have failed to do so. Bearing this in mind, sceptics and ultra-critics will set themselves a hard task should they still persevere in trying to destroy a hoary tradition based upon such pertinent facts as our author has so well succeeded in marshalling together in this relatively small publication.

It has been admitted by the best authorities that it was by no means difficult for St. Thomas to find his way to Southern India by way of the Persian Gulf, or the Red Sea, even if he could not have done so overland. Roman vessels were plentiful in those days both in

Malabar and Ceylon. Their route was the Red Sea—which the Romans easily reached from Alexandria. Numerous gold and silver coins from the time of Augustus Cæsar have recently been un-earthed in Malabar and Ceylon. These facts again suggest the possibility of St. Thomas having followed the Roman route to India *via* the Red Sea. And the fact that the Island of Socotra claims to have been evangelised by this Apostle is significant. In this connection again the following words quoted from an April number of the "Madras Times" 1915, relating to a collection of such coins in the Madras Museum will be read with interest :—

"It is wonderful testimony to the extent of the Roman Empire that out here in India there should be so many finds of old Roman coins. *Mr. Desikachariar* tells us that for a period dating from Augustus, whose reign included the year 1 of the Christian era, there was considerable commercial intercourse between South India and Rome. In the luxurious days of the Emperors, treasures were imported from all parts of the world into the great city. It is interesting to wonder whether these coins at the Museum were the price of peacocks supplied for the glorification of a Cæsar's wife."

"Roman intercourse with India was such that a force of Roman cohorts was stationed on the Malabar Coast to protect Roman trade and it is thought possible that the supplies of Roman coins in India may have been minted locally for the convenience of the large colony of Roman merchants and Roman soldiers in India and Ceylon."

"*Tyler Denett* again while describing the Romantic History of Ameradhapura—the dream city of Ceylon in the *New York Tribune*, says that Roman coins—a few gold ones and many of copper—have been found in the ruins of other cities. Doubtless the Singalese maintained commercial relations with the Romans for centuries after Constantinople was established."

The thanks, therefore, and gratitude of the Diocese of St. Thomas of Meliapur are due to the author for his patient study, research, and endeavour in bringing out a publication which in a few pages throws more light perhaps on the subject than volumes of others have done. The thanks are his too—of all the lovers of this fiery Apostle whose own doubt of Christ's Resurrection from the Dead affords us the surest proof of it,--of that Apostle, I say, who went forth into the farthest ends of the earth preaching his Risen Lord and God. I have no doubt this little volume will appeal to the learned—besides being of interest to the general reader—and to the many pilgrims in particular, as well as tourists, who from all parts of the world constantly visit the Apostle's Shrines at the San Thomé Cathedral, the "Little Mount", and St. Thomas' Mount, with which the history of modern Madras is so intimately bound up.

SAN THOME DE MELIAPUR,
FEAST OF ST. THOMAS, APOSTLE,
21st December 1921.

A. M. TEIXEIRA,
Vicar-General and Administrator of the Diocese of Mylapore.

THE OLD CATHEDRAL, SAN THOMÉ. DEMOLISHED IN 1893.
TOMB OF ST. THOMAS THEN IN THE DOMED ORATORY AT THE BACK.
NOW IN TRANSEPT OF THE NEW CATHEDRAL.

ST. THOMAS, THE APOSTLE, IN INDIA.

PART I.

ST. THOMAS IN THE BIBLE AND TRADITION.

I. THE BIBLE RECORD.

No incident is recorded of St. Thomas, the Apostle, in the synoptic Gospels. Only his name is mentioned with the others in the lists given by Matthew (x. 3), Mark (iii. 18) and Luke (vi. 15). In the Gospel of St. John, however, he appears in a characteristic light, and is revealed as a personality of singular charm and interest, full of devotion and ready to die with his Lord and Master. It was when Jesus was going to Judæa to raise Lazarus to life, where the Jews had lately sought to stone Him, and the rest of the disciples endeavoured to dissuade Him from making that journey, that St. Thomas, who is here called Didymus (twin), said: "Let us also go that we may die with Him." (John, xi. 16). So great was his love for his Divine Master even before the descent of the Holy Ghost. Again, when our Lord at the Last Supper informed his disciples that He was about to leave them, but told them for their comfort that He was going to prepare a place for them in His Father's House, and whither he was going they knew and the way they knew, St. Thomas, who ardently desired to follow Him, said: "Lord, we know not whither thou goest; and how can we know the way?" Christ at once quieted his misapprehension by replying: "I am the way, the truth, and the life: no man cometh to the Father, but by me." (John, xiv. 2-6). After His resurrection, when our Lord appeared to His disciples, Thomas was not with them, and would not credit their statement that they had seen the Lord. " Except I see in his hands," he said, " the print of the nails and put my finger into His side, I will not believe." He evidently presumed that it was a mere phantom or apparition. After eight days when the disciples were again assembled and Thomas was with them, Jesus appeared and stood in their midst, although the doors were shut, and said : " Peace be to you." Then addressing Thomas, He said : " Put in thy finger hither and see my hands. And bring hither thy hand and put it into my side ; and be not faithless but believing." Thomas answered and said to Him : " My Lord and my God." Jesus then said to him : " Because thou hast seen me, Thomas, thou hast believed : blessed are they that have not seen and have believed." (John, xx. 20--29). Notwithstanding this gentle rebuke of our Lord, the very circumstance of St. Thomas's incredulity at first and subsequent confession of faith in the reality of the Resurrection and of the Divinity of Christ, is held by the Fathers of the Church as having done more to confirm us in our faith in those fundamental truths of Christianity than the belief of all the other Apostles. St. Thomas was present again when our Lord appeared once more to his disciples by the sea of Tiberias (John, xxi. 2) ; and he is mentioned for the last time in the Acts of the Apostles (i.13-14) when, after the Ascension of Christ into Heaven, Thomas is said to have been in an upper room in Jerusalem with the other Apostles, " persevering with one mind in prayer with the women and Mary the mother of Jesus and with his brethren." This is all that can be gathered from the Bible regarding Thomas, the Apostle.

ST. THOMAS' MOUNT.

II. THE TRADITION.

As regards his subsequent career, tradition has it, to take the summary given in the *Roman Breviary*, that the Apostle Thomas, who was also called Didymus, a Galilean, after receiving the Holy Ghost, went to many countries to preach the Gospel of Christ; that he handed over the precepts of the Christian faith and life to the Parthians, the Medes, the Persians, the Hircanians and the Bactrians; that finally betaking himself to the Indians he instructed them in the Christian religion; that when towards the end, by the sanctity of his life and doctrine and the greatness of his miracles, he aroused in all others admiration for himself and love for Jesus Christ, he greatly excited to anger the King of that nation, a worshipper of idols; and being condemned by his sentence and pierced with arrows, he adorned the honour of the Apostolate with the crown of martyrdom at Calamina. This is supplemented by the information recorded in the *Roman Martyrology*, where it is further stated that his relics were first translated to Edessa (now called Urfa or Orfa, a City of Northern Mesopotamia on a tributary of the Euphrates) and then to Ortona in Central Italy on the Adriatic. Then there is the long-accepted belief that he not only visited the north of India, but also preached in Southern India, where he established churches and left congregations known to this day as the St.Thomas' Christians, and that in the end he was martyred in St. Thomas' Mount and buried in San Thomé, now a suburb of Madras. And thus the glory of the introduction of Christianity in India has, by time-honoured tradition, been ascribed to St. Thomas, the Apostle.

PART II.

THE DISCUSSION.

I. CONNECTION WITH INDIA.

The question of St. Thomas's connection with India has been a subject of perennial interest, and quite a considerable amount of literature has grown around it. Mr. Vincent Smith in his *Oxford History of India*, 1919, remarks, that " the subject has been discussed by many authors from every possible point of view, and immense learning has been invoked in the hope of establishing one or other hypothesis, without reaching any conclusion approaching certainty." And he adds : " There is no reason to expect that additional evidence will be discovered." It may be that fresh evidence will never be discovered to confirm with certainly the time-honoured tradition as we have it now. But is it the case that Mr. Vincent Smith himself has made the best of what evidence we have ? It is hoped that the present investigation will show that the evidence already available is even stronger in support of the tradition connecting St. Thomas with Southern India than Mr. Vincent Smith has allowed, and that those writers who are disposed to confine the Apostle's labours to the north of India are by no means justified in doing so.

The most comprehensive research on this subject is contained in that volume, published in 1905, entitled, " India and the Apostle Thomas," by Dr. A. E. Medlycott, at one time Vicar Apostolic of Trichur in the Cochin State. And yet it is curious to note that Dr. Burkitt in his article on St. Thomas in the *Encyclopædia Britannica* makes the remark that Dr. Medlycott's *India and the Apostle Thomas* is wholly uncritical, and Father Thurston in the bibliography attached to his article on the same subject in the *Catholic Encyclopedia* merely echoes the statement by referring to Dr. Medlycott's book, as a work written by a Catholic Vicar Apostolic, but uncritical in tone. Neither of these writers, however, assigns any reason for so sweeping a statement. As the ordinary reader will naturally go to the *Encyclopædia Britannica* or the *Catholic Encyclopedia* for some short condensed information on the subject, it is well to inquire how far the articles in them can be relied upon, and how far their authors are justified in maintaining as against Dr. Medlycott that, while there is evidence to show that St. Thomas preached in the north of India, there is not sufficient evidence to support the tradition connecting the Apostle with Southern India.

As against the sweeping condemnation of Dr. Medlycott's work referred to, it would suffice to cite the opinion of the writer (J. Kennedy), who reviewed Dr. Medlycott's work in the *Journal of the Royal Asiatic Society* for October 1906. This writer says: "In many respects he is well fitted for his task. He has a knowledge of Syriac, and is acquainted with the local legends of Mylapore, and the latest researches of Indian scholars, as well as of English and German students of the Apocrypha. He brings an immense mass of material to the discussion—the Epitaph of Abercius, the Acts of Paul and Thekla, of Andrew, and of Archelaus; he gives the history of the Apostle's relics; and he goes through the evidence for an Indian Church before the days of Cosmas Indicopleustes. Moreover, he has given as his own special contribution to the subject extracts from the Church calendars and sacramentaries." And again when concluding his review Mr. Kennedy remarks: "If we are seldom convinced by the Bishop's arguments, we are thankful to him for the fullness of his materials and the antidote he offers to the ultra-sceptical position of Milne Rae." Thus, while refusing to accept some of Dr. Medlycott's conclusions, Mr. Kennedy does not grudge to acknowledge that he was well fitted for his task. Besides, as Mr. Vincent Smith also testifies, Dr. Medlycott's book "supplies an invaluable collection of ecclesiastical texts" and "is full of abstruse learning." We can have no hesitation, therefore, in drawing upon Dr. Medlycott's materials, among others, for our present investigation, without accepting all he has to say on the subject.

The fault in Dr. Medlycott is that he is too diffuse, and "full of abstruse learning," as Mr. Vincent Smith has remarked, and he lays more stress on minor points than is necessary, and thus diverts the mind from the main issues. His object was to bring together a mass of evidence, not only to establish the truth of the tradition, but also to show that there was a persistent and constant tradition in the Church connecting the Apostle with Southern India. It is his method that has made it difficult for some critics to follow him.

The Rev. George Milne Rae, referred to by Mr. Kennedy, was once a Professor of the Christian College, Madras. He published a book in 1892 on *The Syrian Church in India*, which is often quoted, and in which he aimed at showing that St. Thomas preached only in that part of India which lies to the west of the Indus and not in the south. The aim of the present essay is to show that there is no justification for confining St. Thomas's labours to the north, and ignoring the weight of the evidence in favour of the Apostle's connection with the south.

A little before Dr. Medlycott published his book, an article appeared in the *Journal of the Royal Asiatic Society* for April 1905 on "St. Thomas and Gondophernes" by J. Fleet, I.C.S. (Retired), Ph.D., C.I.E. The writer here summed up the results of an investigation undertaken by Mr. W. R. Philipps in the *Indian Antiquary* (1903) from Western sources of information, and supplemented Mr. Philipps' work by an examination of an item obtained from Eastern sources by way of corroboration of the Western tradition. Dr. Burkitt considers that the best investigation of the traditions connecting St. Thomas with India is that by W. R. Philipps in the *Indian Antiquary,* while Father Thurston refers to Dr. Fleet's article as "his severely critical paper." We cannot do better, therefore, than begin with these authorities, and then turn to Dr. Medlycott and other sources as we proceed with the subject.

In the meantime it must be observed that Dr. Philipps himself in drawing up the *General Conclusions* arrived at as a result of his researches, put them forward as tentative, as he hoped that Dr. Medlycott, who was then writing his volume, would afford us some fresh information, especially from recently explored syriac sources. How far Dr. Medlycott has succeeded in throwing further light on the matter will be seen from our present investigation.

However, Dr. Fleet says that Mr. Philipps has given us an exposition of the Western traditional statements up to the sixth century A.D. and that one decidedly important feature of his result is that they make it quite clear, even to those who have not specially studied the matter, that we are not in any way dependent upon apocryphal writings or upon certain later works which he specifies, as the tradition goes back to much more ancient times and is based upon far better authority. And taking only some of the most ancient statements, Dr. Fleet finds that, in its earliest traceable form, the tradition runs thus :—

According to the Syriac work entitled, *The Doctrine of the Apostles*, which was written, he says, in perhaps the second century A.D., St. Thomas evangelised "India." St. Ephraem, the Syrian (born about A.D. 300, died about 378), who spent most of his life at Edessa in Mesopotamia, states that the Apostle was martyred in "India," and that his relics were taken thence to Edessa. That St. Thomas evangelised the Parthians is stated by Origen (born A.D. 185 or 186, died about 251—254). Eusebius (Bishop of Cæsarea Palæstinæ from A.D. 315 to about 340) says the same. And the same statement is made by the "Clementine Recognitions," the original of which may have been written about A.D. 210.

A fuller tradition, he says, is found in *The Acts of St. Thomas*, which exists in Syriac, Greek, Latin, Armenian, Ethiopian and Arabic, and in a fragmentary form in Coptic. And this work connects with St.Thomas two Eastern Kings, whose names appear in the Syriac version as Gudnaphar, Gundaphar, and Mazdai. The Syriac version of the Acts, he says, may be regarded as the original one, and as more likely than the others to present fragments of genuine history. It dates back, according to Dr. Wright to not later than the fourth century ; while Mr. Burkitt would place the composition of it before the middle of the third century, and Lipsius would seem to have placed it in or about A.D. 232. Harnack, according to Fr. Thurston in the *Catholic Encyclopedia*, assigns to it even an earlier date, before A.D. 220.

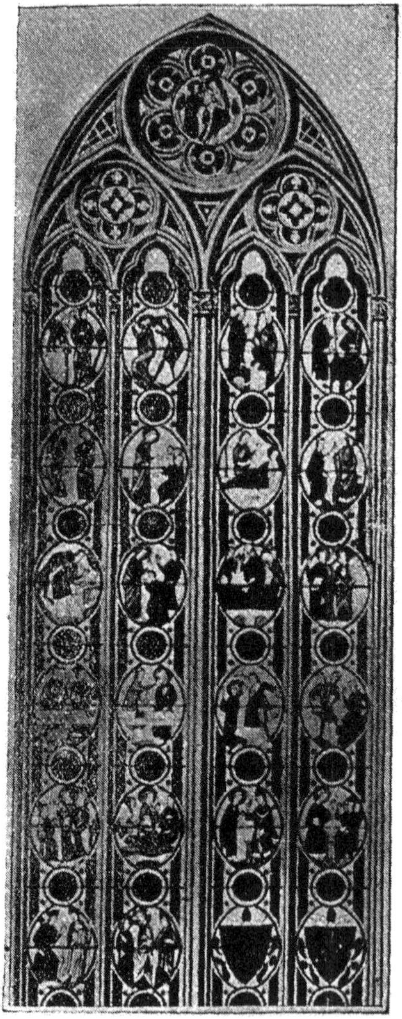

STAINED GLASS, CATHEDRAL, TOURS, FRANCE.

(See *Explanation* p. v.)

The substance of the tradition as gathered from the *Acts* according to Dr. Fleet is as follows :—

On the occasion when the twelve Apostles divided the countries of the world among themselves by lot, 'India' fell to St. Thomas. He did not wish to go there. But a merchant named Habban had been sent into " the southern country " by Gudnaphar, " King of India," to procure for him a skilful artificer. Our Lord appeared to Habban and sold St. Thomas to him for twenty pieces of silver. St. Thomas and Habban started next day. Travelling by ship they came to a place named Sandaruk. There they landed and attended the marriage feast of the King's daughter. Thence they proceeded into " India" and presented themselves before King Gudnaphar. And there St. Thomas preached in the cities and villages, and converted the King himself and his brother and many other people. After that, while St. Thomas was preaching "throughout all India," he went to the city of King Mazdai. There, as the result of his converting Mazdai's wife Tertia and a noble lady named Mygdonia, he was condemned to death. He was slain with spears by four soldiers on a mountain outside the city. And he was buried in the sepulchre in which the ancient kings were buried. But subsequently, while King Mazdai was still living, the bones of the Apostle were secretly removed by one of the brethren and were taken away to " the West."

The Greek, Latin, and other versions give sundry additional details, besides presenting variants of the names of the persons and places. However, the important point is, as Dr. Fleet remarks, that a Christian tradition, current in Syria, Palestine, Egypt, Asia Minor, and all those parts as far as Italy, and connecting St. Thomas with Parthia and "India" and with two "Indian" Kings whom it specifically names, is traceable back to, at any rate, the third or fourth century of the Christian era, and perhaps to the second quarter of the third century. But as the Christian tradition taken in its details and in its external bearings would seem to require corroboration of some kind or other from external sources, the required corroboration has been found in coins which from 1834 onwards have been obtained from Beghram in the vicinity of Kabul, from Pathankot in the Gurdaspur district of the Punjab on the north-east of Amritsar, from Kandahar, and from various places in Sindh and Seistan, bearing the name of one of the Kings, Gondopheres, mentioned in the tradition. But again as these coins are not dated and there was further wanted an epigraphic record which should present a date in some era, capable of being recognized as a date of Gondopheres, and adaptable to the tradition, it has happened that the desideratum was at length supplied by the discovery, in or about 1857, of what is known as the Takht-i-Bahi inscription, which is now in the Lahore Museum.

We need not pursue the investigation undertaken by Dr. Fleet in connection with the coins and the inscription. It is sufficient to note that the result, placing the commencement of the reign of Guduphara-Gondophernes in A.D. 20 or 21, and establishing the fact that in A.D. 46 his dominions included, in India itself, at any rate the territory round about Peshawar, is, as remarked by Dr. Fleet, reached from the Takht-i-Bahi inscription and the coins, without any help from the Christian tradition; while as regards the tradition itself, it gives us, in just the period for the death of St. Thomas, a King, Guduphara-Gondophernes, whose name

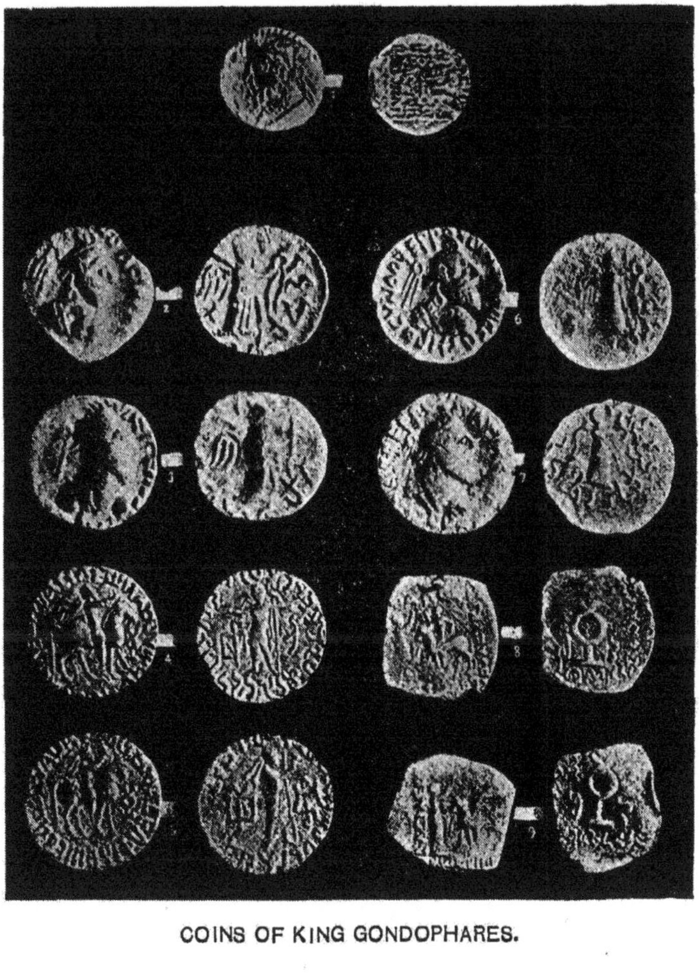

COINS OF KING GONDOPHARES.

can be satisfactorily identified with that of the Gudnaphar, Gundaphar, Goundapharos, and Gundaforus of the tradition, and who would be quite properly mentioned as a King of India or of the Indians, so that Dr. Fleet naturally concludes that the evidence so far is at least strongly suggestive of the fact "that there is an actual basis for the tradition in historical reality, and that St. Thomas did proceed to the East, and visited the courts of two kings reigning there, of whom one was the Guduphara-Gondophernes of the Takht-i-Bahi inscription and the coins," who, judging from the wide range of the localities from which the coins were obtained, was evidently the powerful ruler "of an extensive territory, which included, as a part of it, much more of India than simply a portion of the Peshawar district."

———

II. IN SOUTHERN INDIA.

Up to this point the best authorities are agreed. It is when they come to locate the territory over which the second King, Mazdai, reigned, the King mentioned in the *Acts of St. Thomas* as the one in whose dominions he brought his apostolic labours to a close by receiving the martyr's crown, that some of them have been led astray. Dr. Fleet thinks that the suggestion made by M. Sylvain Levi to take the name Mazdai as a transformation of a Hindu name, made on Iranian soil and under Mazdean influences, and arrived at through the forms Bazadeo, Bazdeo, or Bazodeo, Bāzdeo, which occur in Greek legends on coins, and to identify the person with King Vasudeva of Mathura, a successor of Kanishka, is not unreasonable; and he accordingly ends his paper by remarking that the other king whom the Apostle visited was very possibly Vasudeva of Mathura.

Now, much depends on the acceptance of this theory of M. Levi; for it follows then that if St. Thomas was put to death in the Kingdom of Mathura in the north, he could not have been martyred at St. Thomas' Mount in the south. It is no surprise, therefore, to find Dr. Fleet making the statement that there is no evidence at all that the place where St. Thomas was martyred was anywhere in Southern India. But Dr. Fleet admits that the question of identifying Mazdai with King Vasudeva of Mathura is not a matter of the same certainty as in the case of King Gondophernes, and that it is possible that some other conclusion might be formed in respect of the name Mazdai, either by means of Persian history or legend or in any other way. In fact Dr. Medlycott puts forward a more reasonable suggestion

STAINED GLASS OVER THE HIGH ALTAR IN THE CATHEDRAL AT SAN THOMÉ.

and we shall presently refer to it, after showing that the theory of M. Levi cannot well be maintained.

Father Thurston in the *Catholic Encyclopedia* following in the wake of Dr. Fleet, whose article in the *Journal of the Royal Asiatic Society*, he refers to, as we said, as a "severely critical paper," also accepted the suggestion of M. Levi, and hence also he naturally finds it "difficult to discover any adequate support for the long-accepted belief that St. Thomas pushed his missionary journeys as far south as Mylapore not far from Madras, and there suffered martyrdom." Apart from the main point, there is a little confusion here in Fr. Thurston's mind. Mylapore is included in Madras. The tradition is that the Apostle was martyred at St. Thomas' Mount near Madras, that is, as the *Acts* say, 'on a mountain outside the city,' and was buried in Mylapore on the sea coast, that particular spot or village being called *San Thome* after the Apostle.

When Dr. Fleet, in his article in the *Journal of the Royal Asiatic Society*, for April 1905, accepted M. Levi's suggestion to identify King Mazdai with King Vasudeva of Mathura in the north, Dr. Fleet, according to his own calculation, allotted B.C. 58 as the commencement of Kanishka's reign, so that Vasudeva who was one of his successors was apparently contemporary with Gondophares; but Dr. Fleet writing subsequently in 1910 in the *Encyclopedia Britannica* (see *Inscriptions, Indian*), while adhering to B.C. 58 as the year when Kanishka began to reign, says that he was succeeded by Vasishka, Huvishka and Vasudeva and that then the dynasty of Kanishka was succeeded by a foreign ruler, Gondophares, who, he adds, is well known to Christian tradition in connection with the mission of St. Thomas, the Apostle, to the East. Thus, according to Dr. Fleet himself, Vasudeva could not have been the King who put the Apostle to death if the latter was alive during the reign of Gondophares, who, as he says, succeeded Vasudeva. Dr. Fleet apparently could no longer support the theory to identify King Magdai with Vasudeva when he wrote in 1910, as he does not say anything in that article as to whether Vesudeva was in any way connected with St. Thomas.

Again, Mr. Vincent Smith, in the third edition of his *Early History of India* published in 1914, not only questioned the correctness of Dr. Fleet's chronology and showed that the relegation of Kanishka to B.C. 58 was wholly out of the question, but placed in that volume the accession to the throne of that monarch in about 78 A.D., remarking that it was possible that the true date might be even later. In his more recent work, *The Oxford History of India*, 1919, he says, " further consideration of the evidence from Taxila now available leads me to follow Sir John Marshall and Professor Sten Konow in dating the beginning of Kanishka's reign approximately in A.D. 120, a date which I had advocated many years ago on different grounds." From this history it appears that Kanishka reigned about forty-two years. Vasishka, mentioned before as Kanishka's immediate successor according to Dr. Fleet, was, Mr. Vincent Smith says, one of his sons and Viceroy, who predeceased the father, who was therefore, really succeeded by Huvishka in A.D. 162, who in turn was succeeded by Vasudeva in A.D. 182, so that according to Mr. Vincent Smith, Vasudeva came too late to be the second king whom the Apostle is said to have visited and by whose orders he was put to death. In either case the suggestion to identify King Mazdai with

Vasudeva of Mathura falls to the ground; and with it the inference based on this theory that St. Thomas was martyred by a king who reigned in the north, and that therefore his martyrdom could not have taken place at St. Thomas' Mount in the south.

As we stated before, Dr. Fleet admitted that the question of identifying Mazdai with King Vasudeva of Mathura in the north was not a matter of the same certainty as in the case of King Gondophares, and that it is possible that some other conclusion might be formed in respect of the name Mazdai, either by means of Persian history or legend or in any other way; and we remarked then, that Dr. Medlycott had in fact put forward a more reasonable suggestion. Having now conclusively shown that the Mazdai-Vasudeva theory is altogether untenable, we shall proceed to examine Dr. Medlycott's suggestion.

Although the point we have investigated did not occur to Dr. Medlycott as he wrote his book in 1905, he discusses the suggestion made by M. Levi on other grounds and shows how far-fetched the idea is to attempt to identify Mazdai with Vasudeva, while as suggested by him there can be nothing unreasonable in identifying the name of the King who was responsible for the martyrdom of St. Thomas with *Mahadeva.* He points out that not only in the north, but also in the south, Indian Kings were in the habit of incorporating the epithet of the divinity with their own names, and instances the fact of one of the rulers of the Warangal dynasty bearing the name of Mahadeva. We may add that a glance at Sewell's *Dynasties of Southern India* shows how common it was for the Kings of the South Indian dynasties to not only affix but also prefix the term *Deva* to their names, and that the name *Mahadeva* itself occurs also among the rulers of other dynasties of Southern India, such as Orissa, Vijayanagar and the Yadavas of Devagiri. It is by no means unreasonable, therefore, to conclude that the name of the King who had St. Thomas martyred was very probably *Mahadeva,* which would be popularly contracted into *Mahdeo.* "Now," remarks Dr. Medlycott, "if the name Mahadeo be passed through Iranian mouths, it will probably assume the form of 'Masdeo,' owing to the similarity of sound with the Iranian name Mazdai, the sibilant would be introduced, and the outcome of Mahadeo or Madeo would be Masdeo, and would appear in Syriac as Mazdai."

Mr. Vincent Smith, again, when he wrote the *second edition* of his *Early History of India* in 1908, was absolutely opposed to the tradition connecting St. Thomas with the Southern India, as a result probably of relying mainly on W. R. Philipps and Milne-Rae; but he considerably modified his views when he published the *third edition* of his history in 1914, and justified the change in his attitude towards it in an appendix embodied in this edition (p. 245). While admitting (p. 234) that "the traditional association of the name of the Apostle with that of King Gondophares is in no way at variance with the generally received chronology of the reign of the latter as deduced from coins and an inscription," he points out that, on the other hand, "there is no trace of the subsequent existence of a Christian community in the dominions which had been ruled by Gondaphares." He allows, however, that "unless a Christian mission connected by tradition with the rite of St. Thomas had visited the Indo-Parthian borderland it is difficult to imagine how the obscure name of Gondophares can have come into the story". Accordingly he thinks that "if anybody chooses to believe that St.

Thomas personally visited the Indo-Parthian Kingdom, his belief cannot be considered unreasonable", as " it is possible that as Dr. Medlycott suggests, he may have first visited Gondophares and then travelled to Southern India." In any case he does not accept the story of the Apostle's *martyrdom* in the north, for he says, " if there be any truth in the tradition that the Apostle was martyred at St. Thomas' Mount near Madras, he cannot possibly have suffered in the Kingdom of Mazdai," taking it for granted that King Mazdai reigned in the north; and he refers here in a footnote, to Father Joseph Dahlmann, S.J., who, he says, " has devoted an ingenious treatise, entitled *Die Thomas Legende und die altesten historischen Beziehungen des Christentums zum fernen Osten im Lichte der indischen Altertumskunde* (Freiburg im Breisgau, 1912), to an attempt to establish the historical credibility of the Gondopharē's story "; adding, " I have read his work carefully without being convinced." We have not read Father Dahlmann's treatise ourselves; but he apparently also accepted the theory that King Mazdai, who put the Apostle to death, was a king who reigned in the north, based evidently on M. Levi's suggestion that Mazdai was possibly Vasudeva of Mathura in the north. It is surprising that it did not occur to Mr. Vincent Smith, while declining to accept the story of the Apostle's martyrdom in the north, to question the theory identifying King Mazdai of the *Acts* with Vasudeva of the north, seeing that his own chronology of the reign of the latter was at variance with the time of the Apostle, and made it impossible for him to accept such a suggestion. Had he noticed this discrepancy, he would probably have been still more emphatic and whole-hearted in his support of the tradition connecting the martyrdom of St. Thomas with

Southern India, than we find he is in the following admissions contained in his latest works :—

"It must be admitted that a personal visit of the Apostle to Southern India was easily feasible in the conditions of the time, and that there is nothing incredible in the traditional belief thathe came by way of Socotra, where an ancient Christian settlement undoubtedly existed. The actual fact of such personal visit cannot be either proved or disproved. I am now satisfied that the Christian Church of Southern India is extremely ancient, whether it was founded by St. Thomas in person or not, and that its existence may be traced back to the third century with a high degree of probability. Mr. Milne-Rae carried his scepticism too far when he attributed the establishment of the Christian congregations to missionaries from the banks of the Tigris in the fifth or sixth century." (*Early History of India*, 1914, p. 235.)

"My personal impression, formed after much examination of the evidence, is that the story of the martyrdom in Southern India is the better supported of the two versions of the saint's death." (*Oxford History of India*, 1919, p. 126).

The bias that has led some of our authorities to confine St. Thomas's labours to the north can further be seen from some absurd and unwarranted inferences drawn by them. Mr. Philipps, for instance, would seem to limit the tracts visited by St. Thomas to the Parthian Empire and to "an 'India' which included the Indus Valley, but nothing to the east or south of it"; and having assumed that the Apostle's tomb must be looked for in Southern Persia, he was driven to the necessity of offering the obviously absurd explanation of the words occurring in the *Acts of St. Thomas*, where he is said to have preached " throughout all India," that " this might imply a number of years" ; that is, words clearly indicating *place and extent* might, it would seem, mean *time* or *period*. Dr. Fleet too, as we have said, apparently under the influence of the Mazdai-Vasudeva theory, is disposed to confine St. Thomas's labours to the north. He premises his investigation by stating that, " whereas the Christian tradition represents St. Thomas the Apostle as the missionary to India and Parthia, by the term ' India ' we are not necessarily to understand simply the country which we now call India. As used by ancient writers, the term denoted the whole of the south-eastern part of Asia, on the south of the Himalaya Mountains, and on the east of a line running from about the centre of the Hindu Kush down along or close on the west of the Sulaiman Range to strike the coast of the Arabian Sea on the west of the mouths of the Indus. It thus included our India, with Burma, Siam, Cochin China, the Malay Peninsula, and the islands of the Indian Archipelago, and with also that portion of Afghanistan which lies between Kabul and Peshawar." And yet, in spite of the evidence before him, he adds : " And the ' India' which is mentioned in the fuller tradition may easily have been a territory of which the principal components lay in Afghanistan and Baluchistan, and which embraced in our India only the Punjab strictly so called and the western parts of Sindh." We noted before that, for the same reason, it was not surprising to find Dr. Fleet making the statement that " there is no evidence at all that the place where St. Thomas was martyred was anywhere in Southern India." He further asserts that "any statement to that effect cannot be traced back beyond the middle ages; and all the real indications point in quite another direction."

Now, if we turn to the following quotation, which Mr. Philipps gives, from the *Doctrine of the Apostles,* we shall see that it more than confirms the statement made in the *Acts of St. Thomas* that he preached "throughout all India," taken in its plain and obvious sense, so that Southern India cannot well be excluded from the range of the Apostle's field of labour. The quotation runs as follows:—

"And after the death of the Apostles there were Guides and Rulers in the churches, and whatever the Apostles communicated to them, and they had received from them, they taught to the multitudes all the time of their lives. They again at their deaths also committed and delivered to their disciples after them everything which they had received from the Apostles, also what James had written from Jerusalem, and Simon from the city of Rome, and John from Ephesus, and Mark from the great Alexandria, and Andrew from Phrygia, and Luke from Macedonia, and Judas Thomas from India; that the epistles of an Apostle might be received and read in the churches, in every place, like those Triumphs of their Acts, which Luke wrote, are read, that by this the Apostles might be known . . ."

"India and all its countries, and those bordering on it, even to the farthest sea, received the Apostles' Hand of Priesthood from Judas Thomas, who was Guide and Ruler in the church which he built there and ministered there."

In the first portion of this extract it will be observed that the name of the Apostle Thomas is connected with India in the same way as Simon (St. Peter) is connected with Rome, and each of the others with the respective places named.

Referring to the original translation by Cureton of the *Ancient Syriac Documents* edited and published by Wright of the British Museum in 1864, from which this quotation is taken, we find that the second portion is one among other similar statements made in connection with other Apostles, where the several countries evangelized by each of them are enumerated in addition to the places specially associated with their names in the first portion of the foregoing extract. The whole account shows the wide range of the field of labour in each case, some of them even overlapping. This being so, it is difficult to imagine how any one can limit the range of St. Thomas's preaching to Northern India, and go to the length of explaining away the words referred to from the *Acts of St. Thomas* as Mr. Philipps has done.

At the same time, it is apparent that Mr. Philipps felt himself the importance of the evidence we have in the *Doctrine of the Apostles*, as he says, it "would be more important if we could fix its date." While admitting that, "from expressions used in it, it is thought to be of the second century", he adds, but Lipsius says 'towards the end of the 4th century, which would bring it to the time of St. Ephraem." Accordingly, he remarks, "apart from this Syriac *Doctrine of the Apostles*" (and we should add, apart also from the *Acts of St. Thomas*, which Burkitt and Harnack place in the beginning of the third century) "there does not seem to be any mention of 'India' in connection with St. Thomas till we get to St. Ephraem (378) and St. Gregory of Nanzienzan (389)"; and he argues that the early evidence then is that St. Thomas evangelized Parthia.

Referring again to Dr. Wright's edition of the *Ancient Syriac Documents* and Cureton's Translation, we find from a note on pages 171-172 against the words, *After the death of the Apostles there were Guides and Rulers in the Church*, that "it would appear from this passage that this treatise must have been written anterior to the time when the title of Bishop, as especially appropriated to those who succeeded to the apostolic office, had generally obtained in the East." Turning then to the note on page 161 against the words, *Guide and Ruler*, we find it stated that "it is plain from the context here, as well as wherever it occurs in these early Syriac documents, that this title is precisely the same as that of Bishop, although the Greek word for it had not obtained in the East. The first mention that we find of the title *Bishop* is in the *Acts of Sharbil*, page 65, about A.D. 105–112, where Barsamya is called the *Bishop of the Christians*, although more generally designated as here." From this, then. it appears that Dr. Cureton would date the document at least early in the second century. Dr. Medlycott, by some inadvertence much to his disadvantage, while dealing with the date of the *Doctrine of the Apostles*, quotes the wrong note (page 147) from the same volume of the *Ancient Syriac Documents*, which refers to the *Doctrine of Addāeus the Apostle*, as having been written notlater than the beginning of the fifth century. And so he argues on different data that the *Doctrine of the Apostles* must be of much earlier date. However, Mr. Philipps apparently saw himself that the *Doctrine of the Apostles* must be of very ancient date ; for, after dealing with the *Acts of St. Thomas*, he goes on to refer to the other writers of the early centuries, and he enumerates them placing the author of the former Syriac work first on the list, adding the words "perhaps 2nd century" ; and he quotes from this document first. Dr. Fleet also evidently saw no reason to dispute this date.

Here, then, we have the authors of *the Doctrine of the Apostles* and of *the Acts of St. Thomas*, belonging to the second and third centuries, respectively, not only attesting to St. Thomas's connection with India, but also to the fact that he preached throughout the country and established himself there, by making himself Guide and Ruler of the church which he built there and ministered there ; and if the writer of *The Clementine Recognitions* and Origen, both of the third century, state that St. Thomas evangelized Parthia, the testimony of the latter, as Mr. Philipps himself says, coming "through the medium of Eusebius," whom he quotes and who belongs to a later century, surely there is nothing here to justify Mr. Philipps' conclusion that St. Thomas was really "the Apostle of the Parthian Empire," and "in some limited sense," the Apostle of India, that is, "probably of an 'India' which included the Indus valley, but nothing to the east or south of it." On the contrary, the whole evidence distinctly supports the tradition that St. Thomas, after preaching the Gospel in Parthia and other countries, and leaving, as we might expect, Guides and Rulers, as they were then called, to continue his mission in those countries, finally betook himself to India, where, as the

Doctrine of the Apostles says, "he was Guide and Ruler in the Church which he built there and ministered there," preaching throughout the country and in those bordering on it even to the farthest seas.

In the face of such evidence how indeed can we exclude Southern India from the scope of St. Thomas's labours and confine him to the north as these authorities have been disposed to do? And what further evidence do we want to establish the very possible connection of St. Thomas with Southern India, when according to Dr.Fleet himself the term "India" as used by ancient writers included so wide a tract as he has described?

However, as if to lend support to the evidence just referred to for the South-Indian apostolate of St. Thomas, we find it related in the Acts that the General, who heard of St. Thomas preaching "throughout all India," came to him in a cart drawn "by cattle"; and Dr. Medlycott points out how travelling in a bullock-cart is characteristic of Southern India, whereas if the incident occurred in the north, the horse would have been introduced on the scene and the General would have been mounted on a steed. Gondophares, for instance, is figured on his coins riding a horse, not seated in a cart drawn by oxen. Further, the fact of Mygdonia using the *palki* or *palanquin* when going to see the Apostle is also specially peculiar to Southern India. Other incidents which strengthen the local colouring given besides those mentioned are also noticed by Dr. Medlycott. The incidents which do not appear to be peculiar to Southern India mentioned by Mr. Philipps are relatively unimportant. In fact Mr. Philipps himself says: "we cannot lay any particular stress upon them in any direction." The objection raised by some critics that certain 'customs' described in the *Acts of St. Thomas* can be shown to be also Biblical and Hebrew, is not to the point , as the comparison made is between the customs peculiar to Southern India and those that prevail in the north.

Further corroborative evidence of a very important nature we find in the testimony of St. Ephraem, A.D. 300 to 378, whose hymns embody the local traditions extant at the time in Edessa. That there was such a tradition then connecting St. Thomas with India, whence his relics were brought to Edessa is not disputed. The actual place of his martyrdom and burial in India is not mentioned by St. Ephraem ; but in one of his hymns written in praise of St. Thomas, he says : " A land of people dark fell to thy lot that these in white robes thou shouldst clothe and cleanse by baptism" ; and in another stanza, " the sunburnt thou hast made fair." At the same time he blesses the merchant who brought so great a treasure as the relics to Edessa, which city in turn he blesses for acquiring and being worthy of possessing this priceless gem, the greatest pearl India could yield. Now, if St. Ephraem believed the relics came from Afghanistan or the north-west corner of India included in the Apostle's time in Gondophares's Kingdom, how could he describe their people as dark or sunburnt, seeing that those regions are more or less in the same latitude as Edessa. The inference, therefore, obviously is that the tradition current in St. Ephraem's time was, that St. Thomas preached mainly in Southern India and was martyred and buried there.

III. DR. MEDLYCOTT ON THE SUBJECT.

We may now follow the general outline of Dr. Medlycott's work; but may note in passing that, of the different forms of the name of the Indian King found in the *Acts of St. Thomas*, the coins and the Takht-i-Bahi inscription, Mr. Fleet uses the form 'Gondophernes' generally, and cites other forms only when literal quotation is necessary, while Dr. Medlycott prefers to use the form 'Gondophares.' In any case it is not of much moment which form is used.

The Acts of St. Thomas, already referred to, Dr. Medlycott points out, form part of a class of writings known as the "Apocryphal Acts of the Apostles." These writings have of late claimed the attention of several scholars both in England and in Germany. Although the Acts have come down to us with interpolations intended to support the gnostic heresies which prevailed in the early days of Christianity, the discoveries made in recent years have made it possible to test the statements contained in them in the light of actual history. Thus Dr. Medlycott found the ground for a critical handling of the *Acts of St. Thomas* already prepared for him; and an elaborate appendix to his book has been devoted to a 'critical analysis' of these Acts, the author's purpose being to show that the principal events narrated in them are based upon historical reality. We have already given Dr. Fleet's version of the tradition as gathered from the Acts.

Dr. Medlycott begins his work by a thorough investigation of the evidence furnished by the coins and the inscription we have referred to as confirming the first portion of the tradition recited in the Acts connecting the Apostle with King Gondophares. He then proceeds to a close

INTERIOR OF CATHEDRAL AT SAN THOMÉ. (A)–TOMB OF ST. THOMAS.

examination of all the available records supplied by the East and West. To collect and bring these together naturally involved long and patient research. The testimonies of St. Ephraem and other Syrian writers, of the Liturgical books and Calendars of the Syrian Church, of the Fathers of the Western Church, of the Calendars, Sacramentaries and Martyrologies of the same Church, and the witness of the Greek and Abyssinian Churches are all laid under contribution and fully discussed. The evidence, much of which is additional to that cited by Mr. Philipps and Dr. Fleet, all go to confirm the truth of the tradition that St. Thomas did suffer martyrdom in *India*, that is India as we know it now. It follows then, as remarked by Dr. Medlycott, that his tomb, if at all, ought to be found in India. A long chain of witnesses extending from the sixth century to the landing of the Portuguese on the shores of India is accordingly produced, attesting to the constant tradition of the Church that the tomb was really at Mylapore. And yet the fact that the tomb of St. Thomas must naturally be found within the limits of India proper, which in itself, as Dr. Medlycott remarks, is an historical aphorism, has met with the strongest opposition ever since the Portuguese announced the discovery of his tomb at Mylapore. This opposition, the learned author adds, came first and chiefly from quarters which must cause an impartial historian, who patiently investigates the whole history of the case, to consider the same as being rather the outcome of *odium theologicum*, than the result of insufficient historical evidence. A plausible excuse for the general feeling of scepticism created by these writers was, in part, Dr. Medlycott thinks, offered by the want of previous historical knowledge shown by the Portuguese authorities and writers in India who claimed to have discovered the body, or the entire remains of the Apostle, coupled with other uncritical details; and once the opposite view arising at first from the doubt regarding the tomb, was taken up and ruthlessly exploited, it was extended to the preaching of the Gospel by the Apostle within the geographical limits of India itself and a widely extending prejudice was formed. It is only in more recent times, when men, indifferent to that *odium*, or guided by their familiarity with, or their long researches in India, approached the subject, that they came gradually, says Dr. Medlycott, to admit the Apostle's mission to India, and to consider the strong historical claim of Mylapore to be the possible site of his martyrdom and burial as not unfounded.

Dr. W. J. Richards, who for thirty-five years was a C.M.S. Missionary in Travancore and Cochin, and who has collected fresh evidence in support of the tradition, in his book *The Indian Christians of St. Thomas* (London 1908), endorses this view, and writes: "Dr. Medlycott says, with a certain amount of truth that it is the *odium theologicum* which has made many writers so ready to doubt the Church traditions assigning Southern India as the mission-field of the Apostle Thomas, and to contradict also the beliefs of the Syrian Christians of Malabar that they themselves are the descendants of the first converts there."

Accordingly after setting forth the available evidence for the Indian Apostolate, Dr. Medlycott brings forward such evidence as upholds for Mylapore the claim to the tomb. St. Gregory, Bishop of Tours, in his "*In gloria Martyrum*," a work which he revised in 590, shortly before his death, recording the testimony of one Theodore who visited the tomb in India, writes:—"Thomas the Apostle, according to the narrative of his martyrdom, is stated to have suffered in India. His holy remains (*corpus*), after a long interval of time, were removed to the city of Edessa in Syria and there interred. In that part of India where they first rested stand a monastery and a church of striking dimensions, elaborately adorned and designed. This, Theodore, who had been to the place, narrated to us." Dr. Medlycott points out that the evidence here clearly implies the existence of a narrative or acts of the martyrdom of the Apostle which declares that he suffered martyrdom in India, the existence of the first tomb of the Apostle, a church of large dimensions covering the Indian tomb, a monastery adjacent, the monks of which no doubt conducted the services at the shrine, the further knowledge that after the remains of the Apostle had remained buried in India for a time they were thence removed to Edessa, and finally that they were buried anew at Edessa. As Dr. Medlycott remarks, these facts embrace all and even more than is necessary to establish the fact of the early knowledge of the existence of the Indian tomb of the Apostle, while they are confirmed by later evidences.

The record of the next visit to the tomb in India is found in the Anglo-Saxon Chronicle, where King Alfred is reported to have sent in 883 an embassy to Rome and also to St. Thomas in India, in fulfilment of a vow made at the time he was besieged by the heathen Danes. Eminent modern writers of English history are quoted as recording the incident as an ascertained fact of history and not as legend. It is further supported by the early chroniclers, whose works have come down to us. Marco Polo and Friar John of Monte Corvino appear to have both visited the tomb about the same time in 1292 or 1293 and their testimonies are brought forward. Although the name of the town is not mentioned by the witnesses referred to, there seems no reason to doubt that the little town, where the body lay, was Mylapore, which alone, in all India, has all along claimed to possess the original tomb of the Apostle.

Thé further witnesses brought forward are the Blessed Oderic of Pordenone (1324–1325), Bishop John de Marignolli (1349), Nicolo de Conti (1425–1430), Amr', son of Mathew, a Nestorian writer (1340) and certain Nestorian bishops, who writing in (1504) to the *Catholicus* of the East, speak of "the houses of St. Thomas in a city on the sea named Meliapur." This brings the record of the Indian Shrine of the Apostle down to the arrival of the Portuguese in India, and shows that the tradition was by no means invented by them; that it was not only locally believed in, but that it was known and testified to from the sixth century onwards by travellers from the West.

Dr. Medlycott then goes into further historical and traditional evidence regarding the Apostle, attesting to the fact that his remains were at a very early period removed from India to Edessa; that during the life-time of St. Ephraem there existed a church at that place named after the Apostle, holding the relics, of which St. Ephraem speaks in the hymns quoted in an earlier chapter by Dr. Medlycott; that some years later another and a larger church in the same city was completed in honour of the Apostle described as the 'Great Church,' or the 'Basilica'; and that to this church the relics were removed with great pomp and ceremony. Dr. Medlycott shows how some writers have confused the second removal of the relics with the first, also the new church with the older one, and in consequence have made out that the translation of the relics from India

SLAB OF CHALCEDONY WHICH COVERED THE APOSTLE'S RELICS AT CHIOS, NOW IN THE CATHEDRAL AT ORTONA, ITALY, SHOWING FIGURE BUST AND GREEK INSCRIPTION, *viz.*, "*AGIOS THOMAS*," SAINT THOMAS.

ALTAR OF ST. THOMAS, CATHEDRAL, ORTONA, ITALY, UNDER WHICH THE APOSTLE'S RELICS REPOSE.

took place at a later date; whereas the second church was completed after St. Ephraem's death which occurred in June 373, and the second removal of the relics took place in the year 394. The evidence adduced goes further to show that the relics of St. Thomas remained at Edessa until the city was sacked and destroyed by the rising Moslem power, and that some of the surviving Christian inhabitants recovered the relics of the Apostle from the ruins of the church and transferred them for safety to an island off the coast of Asia Minor that of Chios in the Ægean Sea. The stone, which covered the remains there and bore the name of the Apostle and bust engraved and is now in the Cathedral of Ortona, attests to the genuineness of the relics. From Chios the relics were removed to Ortona in 1258. While at Ortona, the relics underwent another vicissitude. The Turks sacked the town in 1566 and burnt and destroyed the churches, including that of the Apostle, whose shrine was exploded by gunpowder. Although the stone forming the altar slab was burst and that of chalcedony brought from Chios was fractured by the explosion, the sacred bones of the Apostle with the relics of other saints were most providentially preserved intact. The head of the Apostle, which was first missed, was found upon further search crushed under the weight of a portion of the fractured altar stone. It was reverently picked up and the skull was reconstructed so thoroughly that no part was found missing. The sacred relics now repose in a bronze urn placed beneath a marble altar, and the head of the Apostle is placed in a silver bust and is exposed to public veneration on the celebration of the feast. The slab of chalcedony marble, which was brought over from Chios and was fractured by the Turks is also preserved in the Church.

IV. THE DOUBT ABOUT THE MARTYRDOM.

In an earlier paragraph we noted that Mr. Vincent Smith, while admitting that his "personal experience, formed after much examination of the evidence, is that the story of the martyrdom in Southern India is the better supported of the two versions of the saint's death," adds that it is by no means certain that St. Thomas was martyred at all, since an earlier writer, Heracleon, the gnostic, asserts that he ended his days in peace. Heracleon, who wrote in the second century, probably about 170 to 180, belonged to Sicily or Italy. St. Clement of Alexandria in his *Stromat*, commenting on the text of Luke, xii. 11, 12, "And when they shall bring you into the synagogues, and to magistrates and powers, be not solicitous how or what you shall answer, or what you shall say; for the Holy Ghost shall teach you in the same hour what you must say," says that Heracleon, the most distinguished of the school of Valentinus, writes, "that there is a confession by faith and conduct, and one with the voice. The confession that is made by the voice and before the authorities, is what the most reckon the holy confession. Not soundly: and hypocrites also can confess with this confession. But neither will this utterance be found to be spoken universally; for all the saved have (not ?) confessed with the confession made with the voice and departed. Of whom are Matthew, Philip, Thomas, Levi and many others. And confession with the lips is not universal, but partial." Mr. Philipps quotes this passage, omitting the bracketted word *not* in the sentence, "for all the saved have not confessed with the voice and departed"; and hence he naturally says it is not particularly intelligible. It is taken from *The Writings of Clement of Alexandria* translated by the Rev. William Wilson, Edinburgh,

1869, Vol. 2, pp. 170 to 171. But Mr. Philipps also remarks that the sense of the passage from Clement of Alexandria is perhaps better given, than by Wilson, in an article on Heracleon by G. Salmon in the *Dictionary of Christian Biography*, etc., Vol. 2, London, 1880, as follows:—

"Men mistake in thinking that the holy confession is that made by the voice before the magistrates; there is another confession made in the life and conversation, by faith and works corresponding to the faith. The first confession may be made by a hypocrite, and it is one not required of all; there are many who have never been called on to make it, as, for instance, Matthew, Philip, Thomas, Levi (Lebbaeus); the other confession must be made by all."

From this it is evident that the omission of the word, "not," in the translation or even in the original, which we have no means of checking, must be a slip of the pen, as the sentence with that word is quite intelligible. Mr. Philipps says that Lipsius attaches importance to it, but that it is not necessary to adopt Lipsius's ideas, and that his theories were impossible. Dr. Medlycott, referring to Dr. Murdock's comment that Clement allows the statement to pass unchallenged, and that he takes this as a proof that he had nothing to allege against it, remarks that Heracleon denies the martyrdom not of one but of several of the twelve Apostles; and that it is not a little surprising that in the light of present day ecclesiastical literature, writers are found to appeal to such an authority in opposition to the common belief of Christendom. Besides, as Mr. J. Kennedy in the *Journal of the Royal Asiatic Society* for October 1906 admits, neither the Western nor the Alexandrian Church was likely to know much of events which had occurred outside the limits of the Roman Empire about the end of the second century. On the other hand the fact of the martyrdom of the Apostle is testified to by the *Acts of St. Thomas*, part at least of which is contemporary with or earlier than Heracleon, and by St. Ephraem (378), St. Ambrose (397), St. Asterius (400), St. Gaudentius (410), St. Gregory of Tours (594), and by later authorities, liturgical books and martyrologies, showing that this has been the constant tradition of the Church.

PORTAL OF THE CHURCH OF "NOTRE DAME," SEMUR, CÔTE D'OR, FRANCE.

V. THE MARTYRDOM.

The different versions of the martyrdom of the Apostle are also set forth and examined by Dr. Medlycott. The narrative, according to the Syriac version of the *Acts of St. Thomas*, is that the King (Mazdai) ordered Thomas to be brought up for judgment, and questioned him as to whence he came and who was his master. The King hesitated what sentence he would pass, or rather how he should compass his death without causing popular excitement, "because he was afraid of the great multitude that was there, for many believed in our Lord and even some of the nobles." So Mazdai took him out of town to a distance of about half a mile and delivered him to the guard under a prince with the order, "Go up on this mountain and stab him." On arriving at the spot the Apostle asked to be allowed to pray, and this was granted at the request of Vizam, the King's son, one of the two last converts. Arising from his prayer, Thomas bid the soldiers approach and said, "Fulfil the will of him who sent you." "And the soldiers came and struck him all together, and he fell down and died." The Greek version and the Latin *De Miraculis* generally agree with the Syriac text, but the Latin *Passio* has a different account. In this version the death of the Apostle occurs at a much earlier period, and was occasioned by the king forcing the Apostle to adore the idol in the temple. When at the Apostle's prayer and bidding the idol was destroyed, the priest of the temple, raising a sword transfixed the Apostle, saying, 'I will avenge the insult to my God.' The local version of the martyrdom prevailing on the Coromandel Coast, as given by Marco Polo and Bishop John de Marignolli, is that St. Thomas while praying in the wood was accidentally shot by an arrow aimed at a peacock. Yet another version of the story, as related by Linschoten, is that, owing to the miracle performed by St. Thomas of removing a log of wood which fell into the mouth of the haven of the town of Mylapore and blocked the traffic, whereby many conversions were made, the Brahmins became his great enemies and sought to bring about his death, which in the end they accomplished by persuading some of the people to stab him on his back while praying in the church. The same narrator states that this incident is found painted and set up in many places and churches in India in memory of the event. There are also other local versions as will be seen later on. However, the old Liturgical Books and Martyrologies of the Nestorian, Latin and Greek Churches, all testify to the fact that the Apostle Thomas won a martyr's crown by being pierced by a lance.

Here Dr. Medlycott takes the opportunity of challenging the statement made by Mr. W. R. Philipps in *The Indian Antiquary* of April 1903, that the learned Orientalist Assemani deemed the Indian relics of St. Thomas a Nestorian fabrication. Dr. Medlycott points out that the statement is misleading, since Assemani in the fourth volume of his learned work, *Bibliotheca Orientalis*, Rome, 1728, covers ten folio pages with his proofs in defence of the Indian Apostolate of Thomas, which he establishes on the authority of the Fathers in reply to Besnage's cavillings; and further adduces evidence from the Liturgical Books of the Syrian Churches including the Nestorian section, and of Syrian writers, both in proof of his Apostolate as well as of his martyrdom in India. But the *corpus* or bones, as Assemani points out, having been transferred from India to Edessa, and Syrian, Greek and Latin writers having, from the fourth century, written of the body of Thomas as having been

RELIQUARY CONTAINING
FRAGMENT OF A BONE AND
POINT OF LANCE,
SAN THOMÉ CATHEDRAL.

REVERSE OF THE RELIQUARY.

removed 'to Edessa of Mesopotamia,' what Assemani really denies is that the body was found by the Portuguese in India; and quite rightly, adds Dr. Medlycott, because the Portuguese on arriving in India, unaware of the historical data now available regarding the remains of the Apostle, assumed that the tomb at Mylapore yet held the entire remains. An admission made by Mr. Philipps in the paragraph previous to the one containing the statement challenged, appears however to have escaped Dr. Medlycott's notice. Mr. Philipps says that the constant tradition of the Church seems to have been that the body was taken to Edessa, that St. Ephraem, as quoted by him, seems to imply that part of the body had been left in India; and yet Mr. Philipps, in the following paragraph of his article, makes the unqualified statement that Assemani deemed the Indian *relics* of St. Thomas a Nestorian fabrication, whereas as shown above all that Assemani denied was that the body was found by the Portuguese on their arrival in India; and this certainly does not exclude the belief by Assemani himself in St. Ephraem's statement that portion of the remains of the Apostle was left behind in India. As a fact the authorities at the Cathedral of San Thomé claim to possess only a very small portion of the relics, consisting of a fragment of a bone and the extreme point of a lance.

VI. THE MALABAR TRADITION.

Dr. Medlycott then gives a summary of the tradition universally accepted by the St. Thomas Christians of the West Coast, and found prevailing in India at the arrival of the Portuguese as reported by their early writers; viz., that St. Thomas landed on the Malabar Coast at Kodangular (Cranganore), that seven Churches were established, that the Apostle then passed from Malabar to the Coromandel Coast, where he suffered martyrdom, and that at some subsequent period a violent persecution raged against the Christians on the Coromandel Coast, compelling many of them to take refuge among their brethren on the West Coast, where they settled down.

He quotes Col. Yule, *Cathay and the Way Thither,* as upholding the Malabar tradition that it was at Cranganore the Apostle landed and first preached there. St. Francis Xavier is also quoted in support of the existence of the belief among the Christians of Socotra at the time of his visit to that Island, that St. Thomas landed on the Malabar Coast and that they themselves were the descendants of the converts made by the Apostle.

Theophilus, the missionary sent by Constantine about the year 354 A.D., is said to have gone, in the course of his missionary journey, from the Maldives to "other parts of India and reformed many things which were not rightly done among them." Dr. Medlycott argues that Malabar, which is but a short sail from the Maldives, must have been included in the "other parts of India" referred to. Mr. Vincent Smith supports Dr. Medlycott in his contention, in his *Early History of India*, 1914, Appendix M., where he remarks

"Dr. Medlycott is, I think, right in holding that Theophilus visited Malabar and found Christians in that region." He also says that "the historical traditions of India and Ceylon when read together seem to carry the evidence for the existence of the Church in Malabar to the third century." And apart from the Ceylon tradition, he says: "I see no reason for hesitating to believe the Indian tradition that Manikka Vasagar visited Malabar and reconverted two families of Christians to Hinduism. The descendants of these families, who are still known as Manigramakars, are not admitted to full privilege as caste Hindus. Some traditions place the reconversion as having occurred about A.D. 270. If that date be at all nearly correct, the Malabar Church must be considerably older. So far as I can appreciate the value of the arguments from the history of Tamil literature, there seems to be good independent reasons for believing that Manikka Vasagar may have lived in the third century. Some authors even place him about the beginning of the second century. If he really lived so early his relation with the Church in Malabar would confirm the belief in its Apostolic origin." As, however, the question of Manikka Vasagar's date is still in dispute we need not rely on this evidence. Besides, as has been shown, we have other independent evidence to support the tradition connecting St. Thomas with Southern India.

VII. THE TRADITIONAL RECORD.

After quoting St. John Chrysostom and the *Gospel of the XII Apostles*, recently recovered from different Coptic papyrus and other texts, and compiled probably not later than in the second century, in support of the tradition that St. Thomas had visited nearly the whole of the inhabited world in the course of his Apostolic career, Dr. Medlycott sums up the traditional record of the Apostle as follows:—

(1) He would have preached through the whole of that tract of country lying south of the Caspian Sea—the 'Mare Hyrcanum' of his days east of the mountain range of Armenia and of the Tigris, down to Karmania in Southern Persia.

(2) It would be during this first Apostolic tour that he came in contact with the north-western corner of India at Gondophares' court.

(3) After the demise of the Blessed Virgin Mary, when according to ecclesiastical tradition, the second dispersion of the Apostles took place, St. Thomas would have commenced his second Apostolic tour. Probably from Palestine he travelled into Northern Africa and thence, preaching through Ethiopia, he passed on to Socotra, where he must have stayed some time to establish the faith. Going thence he would have landed on the West Coast of India.

(4) From Malabar the Apostle would find no difficulty in crossing over to the Coromandel Coast.

(5) It would be on the Coromandel Coast that he ended his Apostolic labours, and this is upheld by the joint traditions of the Coromandel and Malabar coasts.

It is indeed interesting to see how the various traditions regarding the Apostle mutually hang together; and

STAINED GLASS, CATHEDRAL,
BOURGES, FRANCE.

(See *Explanation* p. vi.)

Dr. Medlycott naturally remarks, how unreasonable it is to suppose that traditions converging from various points mutually self-supporting, can be the outcome of legendary imaginings. It is for those, he adds, who contest them to prove that they are inconsistent with any known facts, and consequently baseless. Until then, he rightly contends, they hold the field.

VIII. CALAMINA.

As regards the name *Calamina*, which is mentioned in some of the writings as the place in India where the Apostle Thomas was martyred, there has been much speculation. Dr. Medlycott refers specially to the article by Mr. Philipps, which we have already alluded to, because, as he says, vague hints are thrown out and 'speculation' indulged in to the effect that 'Caramana', our modern Karman in southern Persia, might represent Calamina. Mr. Philipps held that 'from a geographical, an ethnical, and indeed as it seems to me, from every point of view', the site of the Apostle's tomb ought to be looked for in that quarter rather than in Southern India. Dr. Medlycott, on the other hand, contends that Calamina never had a geographical existence, that the name does not appear in any of the older writings treating of the Apostle, while where it is mentioned, it is added that it is situated in India. India, then, and Southern India we should say, considering the evidence we have already adduced, is the country where we should look for the tomb of St. Thomas. What place is there in India, asks Dr. Medlycott, other than Mylapore, which has ever set forth a claim to it? Decidedly none: in no other part of India, nor elsewhere, has such a claim been raised—that of Edessa was for a second tomb where the sacred remains rested after removal from India. Why, then, should there be any objection to its being placed in Southern India, and topographically at Mylapore, especially as Mr. Philipps himself admits, 'there is nothing inherently improbable in such a supposition'? As to 'Carmana' or Carmania of old, now Karman, Dr. Medlycott further points out that the Nestorians who had churches, priests and Christians in that part of Persia down to past the middle of the seventh century, must certainly have known if at any time it held the Apostle's tomb; that a claim so much nearer home would not have been overlooked by them; and they certainly would not have come to India to search for it. Quotations are given from a letter of the Nestorian patriarch, Jesuab, A.D. 650—660, addressed to Simeon, Bishop of Ravardshir, the Metropolitan of Persia at the time, to show how groundless the suggestion put forward by Mr. Philipps is. Dr. Medlycott however remarks: "We owe it in fairness to the writer of the paper to add that having received from us a copy of the above passages, he reproduced them by way of rectification in a Note published in the *Indian Antiquary*, 1904, page 31, under the heading *Miscellanea*. This phase of the question may now be considered closed."

Gutschmid, again, held the view that Calamina must be identified with Calama on the seaboard of Gedrosa, pointing out that Calama was in the time of the Apostle, under the sceptre of Gandopheres. On the face of it this view is quite untenable as the Apostle was put to death under the orders of quite another King named Mazdai, and the place of his martyrdom must have been under the sceptre of the latter and not of the former.

Dr. Medlycott himself goes further into the subject. He observes that the name does not appear in any of the older authentic writings treating of the Apostle. It appears first in a group of mostly anonymous writings in Greek, which give a brief summary of the doings, preachings and deaths of the Apostles. From this class of writing to which scholars have not been able to assign a date, the supposed authors, Sophronius, a friend of St. Jerome, Hippolytus, Dorotheus and another are quoted as mentioning *Calamina in India* as the place of St. Thomas's martyrdom. From these writings again the name appears to have been taken up by some Syrian writers, and to have made its way into the later Martyrologies.

Some scholars have tried to discredit the authority of these anonymous writings; but where is the object of discrediting them if at the same time attempts are made to identify Calamina with some place outside India. It is a significant fact that no tradition of any kind has been traced as having existed at any time in Northern India, Afghanistan, Beluchistan, Persia or Arabia, connecting the martyrdom and burial of the Apostle with any place in those regions.

Dr. Medlycott is inclined to regard the name Calamina, as fictitious, and ventures on a suggestion as to how it did get connected with the Apostle in the minds of the writers referred to, as the place of his martyrdom in India. Dr. Medlycott thinks that Calamina is probably a compound of the word *Kalah*, the name of a port, the existence of which in the vicinity of India is historically beyond a doubt, and *elmina* which in Syriac denotes a port. Dr. Macleane, in the *Manual of the Administration of the Madras Presidency*, suggests that *Calamina* may be a corruption from Coromandel. This is the name of a small village on the coast north of Madras, which has come to be applied to the Eastern Coast of the Peninsula of India. There is also the suggestion in *Hobson Jobson* by Col. Yule and Dr. Burnell, that the name is in fact *Choramandalam*, the Realm of *Chora*, this being the Tamil form of the very ancient title of the Tamil Kings who reigned at Tanjore. The name also occurs in the forms *Cholamandalam* or *Solamandalam* on the great Temple inscription of Tanjore (11th century) and in an inscription of A.D. 1101 at a temple dedicated to Varahaswami near Seven Pagodas. It is not unlikely that *Calamina*, as mentioned by the old writers, was originally meant for the coast on which the town where the Apostle was martyred was situated. The suggestion, however, put forward in the *Catholic Encyclopedia*, Vol. XIII, page 382, by the late Rev. James Doyle, who was for sometime Editor of the *Catholic Register*, the organ of the diocese of San Thomé, is much to the point. He finds it far more reasonable to believe that *Calamina* was an ancient town at the foot of the hill, St. Thomas' Mount, that has wholly disappeared, as many more recent historic Indian cities have done. This much is certain as he says, till the Europeans settled in the place there was no Indian name even for the hill. This appears from the present Indian name Faranghi Malai (*i.e.*, the hill of the Franks) which is used to denote both the hill and the town around its base, a service which the English name St. Thomas Mount equally fulfils.

IX. MYLAPORE.

As to *Mylapore*, Dr. Medlycott tries to identify it with Ptolemy's *Manarpha* or *Maliarpha*. Of the different texts examined by the author the latter form preponderates, and Dr. Medlycott argues that the form *Maliarpha* contains the two essential ingredients of the name Maliapur, which would be the form known or reported to the Greek geographers. A Greek desinence, as customary in such cases, has evidently been introduced, so in place of *pur* or *phur* (which may represent a more ancient form of pronunciation) we have the Greek termination *pha*; nor has the sound *r* of the Indian name disappeared, for it has passed to the preceding syllable of the word. He adds that if we take into consideration the inaccurate reproduction of Indian names in Ptolemy's present text, it is almost a surprise that so much of the native sound of the name is yet retained. It must be admitted that the name, Mylapore, is not mentioned by other writers until about the fifteenth century. The fact, however, that the maps illustrating Ptolemy's geography place *Maliarpha* where the present Mylapore would be shown is much in favour of Dr. Medlycott's view. The same identification was suggested previously by D'Anville, the French geographer of the eighteenth century (*Georgaphie Ancienne Abregie*, Paris, 1788); as also by Paulinus à Sto. Bartholomeo, the Carmelite missionary of the West Coast (*India Orientalis Christiana*, Romae, 1794).

Col. Love in his *Vestiges of Old Madras* supports this view, and says that Mylapore is generally considered to be the *Malli-arpha* of Ptolemy, and that the original designation of the Portuguese settlement was San Thomé de Meliapur. Hunter in the *Imperial Gazetteer of India* states that the name *Mylapur* is spelt variously—*Mayilapuram*, or

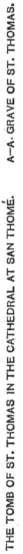

THE TOMB OF ST. THOMAS IN THE CATHEDRAL AT SAN THOMÉ. A—A. GRAVE OF ST. THOMAS.

Peacock town; *Mulaipuram*, or Mount Town; *Meliapur, Mirapur* (by the Portuguese); and *Meelapur in the Tohfatal Majohudin;* that it has been suggested that it is the *Malifattan* of Rashid-ud-din, but that more recent inquirers favour the identification of Negapatam with *Malifattan.* Dr. Macleane in his *Manual of the Administration of the Madras Presidency* gives the derivation of Mylapore from *mayil*, Tamil for peacock, and *pura*, Sanscrit for city, with reference, according to the Brahmins, to the tradition that Parvaty worshipped her husband Shiva in the form of a peacock. According to the local Christian tradition the name would seem to be similarly derived, but with reference to the story ascribing the death of St. Thomas to an arrow aimed at one of the peacocks which were about him while praying in the wood and testifying to the fact that peacocks were plentiful in the locality then.

Dr. Medlycott lays special stress on the *Malabar* tradition in support of the claim of Mylapore to hold the tomb of the Apostle. He is thoroughly convinced even quite apart from all the evidence previously adduced that if the claim of Mylapore to be the place of the martyrdom and of the burial of the Apostle was not based on undeniable fact, the Christians of Malabar would never have acknowledged their neighbours' claim to hold the tomb of the Apostle, neither would they ever be induced to frequent it by way of pilgrimage. Further had this been a case of fictitious claim put forth to secure public notoriety and importance, they would, Dr. Medlycott adds, as probably have, any way, set up one for themselves and would have certainly ignored the claim of the former.

Mr. J. Kennedy in *The East and The West*, April 1907, admits that a considerable amount of truth underlies the legend of St. Thomas's Apostleship, that the shrine at Mylapore had been for many centuries in existence when it was visited by Marco Polo, and that the mention of the miraculous log makes it certain that the shrine Theodore visited in the sixth century was Mylapore. But he is wholly sceptical as to the tomb at Mylapore being the real tomb of the Apostle, as he would confine him to Parthia and the Indus valley, losing sight of the evidence brought forward above, which clearly shows that he cannot reasonably do so. Accordingly, he goes to the length of suggesting that "the discovery of the tomb of St. Thomas on the summit of a wooded hill far from the habitations of men and from all other Christian communities, must certainly have been the work of some Christian hermit," since, as he makes out, in the early ages "both in the East and the West the discovery of wonder-working graves was almost entirely the work of these wandering ascetics," (hermits and monks) who played a great part in the diffusion of Eastern Christianity, especially in the wilder districts." Apart from the inaccuracy of the statement that the tomb was discovered on the top of a hill, whereas it is located in a suburb of Madras on a level with it, the assumptions contained in the statement that it was far from the habitations of men and from all other Christian communities, are too glaring to need even notice. "Western saints, in the centuries immediately succeeding Constantine," he says, "had frequent occasion to expose the claims of so-called martyrs' tombs to superstitious veneration, nor is it less the duty of the modern historian." Just so: and this has been the attitude of the Church all through. But to assert that because in the early ages miracles were related as having occurred in connection with the tombs of saints, and in some cases they have been proved to be spurious, that in this case the discovery of the tomb *must certainly* have been the work of a hermit, is surely not historical criticism. To talk, besides, as he does, of "the worship of wonder-working tombs" and of the veneration of the tomb of St. Thomas at Mylapore as a Christian example of the Pagan cult prevailing throughout India, shows strong anti-Catholic bias. Catholics who venerate the tomb are not compelled to believe in its genuineness; and they know well that it is a question of evidence and they may be mistaken as to the fact. They regard it, in any case, in the light of a memorial, whereby the saint is remembered and honoured. If miracles are said to have occurred in connection with the reputed tomb or relics, Catholics understand again that here also it is a question of evidence, and that, if genuine, they are the result of faith excited by the memorial of the saint, whose intercession had been implored by clients for Divine interposition on their behalf.

X. CONCLUSIONS.

To sum up, the weight of evidence and probability would seem plainly to support the following conclusions :—

(1) That St. Thomas did visit and preach the Gospel in *India*, that is, India as we know it now ;

(2) That as two very ancient documents, such as the *Doctrine of the Apostles* and the *Acts of St. Thomas* state, one, that " India and all its countries and those bordering on it, even to the farthest sea, received the Apostle's hand of Priesthood from Judas Thomas, who was Guide and Ruler in the Church which he built there and ministered there," and the other, that the Apostle preached " throughout all India", and as St. Ephraem refers to the people of the land, which fell to the lot of St. Thomas, as " dark " and " sunburnt ", while Dr. Fleet admits that the term " India " as used by ancient writers included the whole of the south-eastern part of Asia on the south of the Himalaya Mountains so as to take in Burma and Siam, Cochin-China, the Malay Peninsula and the Indian Archipelago, there is no reason why Southern India should be excluded from the field of the Apostle's labours as some writers have endeavoured to do, in the face of such evidence and in spite of the persistent traditions connecting St. Thomas with it ;

(3) That the Apostle did visit the Courts of two Kings reigning in India, one of whom may be taken for certainty to be *Gondophares* in the North, while the other mentioned in the *Acts* as *Mazdai* may reasonably be identified with *Mahadeva*, a name common enough among Kings of the South Indian dynasties, since the suggestion to identify King Mazdai with Vasudeva of Mathura, who, as we have

shown, was not contemporary with St. Thomas, cannot now be maintained ;

(4) That it may be taken, therefore, that the Apostle was martyred in Southern India "outside the City " and " on a mountain," as related in the *Acts*, and that St. Thomas' Mount and Mylapore are the only places which have been identified with the *mountain* and *city* where the Apostle was matyred and buried. by a persistant tradition, the like of which cannot be traced as having ever existed in connection with any other place or places in India or elsewhere :

(5) That his remains were at a very early period removed from India to Edessa, thence to Chios and finally to Ortona, where they now repose ;

(6) That, as at the original removal part of the remains were left behind in India as appears from St. Ephraem, the relics still preserved in an ancient reliquary in the Cathedral at St. Thomé may, not unlikely, be parts of the relics left in the tomb.

PART III.

SOME MINOR OBJECTIONS.

I. INDIA OF THE ANCIENTS.

Some critics, losing sight of the evidence we have brought forward, suggest that as some authorities mention Parthia as the country evangelized by St. Thomas, and others India, the term 'India' had a vague signification in ancient times. They fail to see that the Apostle might easily have been connected with both, as is narrated in the tradition preserved in the Roman Breviary and the Roman Martyrology, that he preached not only to the Parthians, but also to the Medes, the Persians, the Hircaneans, and the Bactrians and finally betook himself to the Indians, where he ended his days by gaining the crown of martyrdom; and that the mention of his connection with one of these countries by any writer need not necessarily be taken to exclude the others, so as to require a forced explanation of the term "India." Again, in connection with the tradition that St. Thomas was martyred at Calamina in India, attempts have been made to include Persia, Arabia and Ethiopia in the India of the ancients and to locate Calamina somewhere outside India proper. We have noted the description given by Dr. Fleet of the India of the ancients, which distinctly excludes Persia, Arabia and Ethiopia from the limits of ancient India; and this is confirmed by an old document like the Bible itself, where a very explicit statement occurs in *Esther* i, 1 regarding Assuerus, who is said to have "reigned from India even unto Ethiopia over one hundred and seven and twenty provinces", showing clearly that a wide tract of country lay between India and Ethiopia. This would exclude not only Ethiopia itself from the India of the ancients, but also Persia, which is mentioned in the same book of the Bible as a separate Kingdom (*Esther* xvi, 14), and Arabia which is spoken of in other books as quite a distinct country (3 Kings x, 15 ; Jer. xxv, 24 ; Gal. i, 17 ; iv, 25).

II. ST. PANTÆNUS.

This being so, Dr. Medlycott's contention that the mission field of St. Pantænus was not the 'India of the Brahmins' as St. Jerome has stated, but Arabia Felix, cannot be upheld. He has been at the pains of trying to prove this, because other writers have put forward the claim of St. Pantænus to be the first missionary who came to India after St. Bartholomew, with the object of rejecting the tradition connecting St. Thomas with it. But if there is quite other independent evidence in support of St. Thomas's connection with India, as Dr. Medlycott himself has shown and as we have further brought forward, how is that evidence in any way weakend by conceding that St. Bartholomew at some time, before or after St. Thomas, did visit some part of India, where he left copies of the Gospel of St. Matthew in Hebrew, one of which St. Pantænus, who was sent from Alexandria to India in the second century, took back with him. The incident is related on the authority of Eusebius, Bishop of Caesarea (A.D. 265—340) and of St. Jerome (A.D. 331 or 340—420); but St. Jerome also connects St. Thomas with India in a way as to convey the unmistakable impression that St. Thomas was known in his days as the real Apostle of India, for he writes of our Saviour that "He was present in all places—with Thomas in India, with Peter in Rome, with Paul in Illyria, with Titus in Crete, with Andrew in Achaia, with each apostolic man in each and all countries." Besides, while, as we have already seen from the *Doctrine of the Apostles*, St. Thomas is connected there with India in a special manner, where, it is said, he was "Guide and Ruler in the Church which he built there and ministered there," it is also stated in that document that the Apostles "visited one another" and "ministered to each other." There should be no surprise, therefore, to find it related that St. Bartholomew also visited India.

The Rev. George Milne Rae in his book *The Syrian Church in India* admits that the India to which St. Pantaenus was sent was certainly not Arabia Felix, as Mosheim seems to have held ; but he endeavours to confine the Saint's missionary labours to northern India, that is, the India, as he says, of Alexander the Great. Of course, his whole aim is to make out that Christianity was not introduced into Southern India until the beginning of the sixth century and then only from the Nestorian patriarchate on the banks of the Tigris by way of the Persian Gulf, and thus to discredit the tradition connecting St. Thomas with Southern India. Accordingly in support of his contention that St. Bartholomew and St. Pantaenus both preached in the North, he makes the assertion that "in the second century," when the latter is reported to have come to India, "there were neither Jews, Christians, nor Brahmins in Malabar," and that the community of Christians of St. Bartholomew, whom he places in the north, were at the end of the second century in so depressed a condition "that they were fain to get help from any quarter, and that perhaps they found it easier, by reason of the regular marine trade with Alexandria, to communicate with the latter than with their own mother Church in Mesopotamia, from which they had long been separated."

Rev. W. J. Richards, for thirty-five years C. M. S. Missionary in Travancore and Cochin, who, since Dr. Medlycott wrote, has collected fresh evidence in support of the tradition connecting St. Thomas with Southern India, shows that there were Jews as well as Brahmins in the Apostolic age in Malabar (*The Indian Christians of St. Thomas*, 1908); while we learn from Vincent A. Smith, a recognized authority on the early history of India, that the Brahmins penetrated into the south many centuries before the Christian era. (*The Oxford History of India*, 1919, page 14.)

As to the suggestion that the moribund Christian community of the north were glad to seek help from Alexandria by reason of the marine trade, rather than from their mother Church in Mesopotamia, which was so much nearer them, it evidently did not occur to Rev. Milne Rae that it really militates against his main contention; for, if it was easier then for the Christian community in the north to be recruited from Alexandria, by reason of the regular marine trade, it must have been just as easy for St. Thomas and St. Pantaenus himself after the former, to have found their way to Southern India, while there is no reason why this part of India should have waited for six centuries, in spite of the facilities afforded by the marine trade, before its turn came to be evangelized, and then too, as Mr. Milne Rae would have it, by Nestorians from the banks of the Tigris by way of the Persian Gulf.

III. THE JEWS.

In connection with the claim to antiquity of the settlement of the Jews in Malabar, the Cochin Census Report, 1901, as quoted by Thurston in *Castes and Tribes of Southern India*, 1909, says that they "are supposed to have first come in contact with a Dradivian people as early as the time of Solomon about B.C. 1000, for 'philology proves that the precious cargoes of Solomon's merchant ships came from the ancient coast of Malabar.' It is possible that such visits were frequent enough in the years that followed. But the actual settlement of the Jews on the Malabar Coast might not have taken place until long afterwards. Mr. Logan, in the Manual of Malabar, writes that 'the Jews have traditions, which carry back their arrival on the coast to the time of their escape from servitude under Cyrus in the sixth century B.C.', and the same fact is referred to by Sir W. Hunter in his 'History of British India.' This eminent historian, in his Indian Empire speaks of Jewish settlements in Malabar long before the second century A.D. A Roman merchant that sailed regularly from Myos Hormuz on the Red Sea to Arabia, Ceylon and Malabar, is reported to have found a Jewish colony in Malabar in the second century A.D. In regard to the settlement of the Jews in Malabar, Mr. Whish observes that "the Jews themselves say that Mar Thomas, the Apostle, arrived in India in the year of our Lord 52, and themselves, the Jews, in the year 69! In view of the commercial intercourse between the Jews and the people of the Malabar Coast long before the Christian era, it seems highly probable that Christianity but followed in the wake of Judaism. The above facts seem to justify the conclusion that the Jews must have settled in Malabar at least as early as the first century A.D."

IV. ECCLESIASTICAL SUPPORT TO THE TRADITION.

Mr. W. R. Philipps, in the article in the *Indian Antiquary*, April 1903, which we have been dealing with, says: "I am not aware that the ecclesiastical authorities at Rome have ever given any real support to the modern belief that St. Thomas was martyred near Madras, and buried at San Thomé or Mylapore; there may be documents in which the idea is mentioned, but never, I think, as a fact established; always with some qualifying phrase so as to leave the question open." If Mr. Philipps had referred to the Bull of Pope Paul V erecting the diocese of San Thomé of Mylapore in 1606, he would have seen that one reason for doing so was "because there lay buried the body of St. Thomas"—There is no qualifying phrase; and it is further emphatically stated that the Holy Father "by the apostolic authority has raised it in perpetuity to, and established it as the city of St. Thomas."

Again Leo XIII in his Apostolic letter dated the 1st September 1886, establishing the Episcopal hierarchy in the East Indies refers to the tradition in the following terms:

"It has been the constant tradition of the Church that the duty of undertaking the discharge of the apostolic office in the vast regions of the East Indies fell to the lot of St. Thomas. He, indeed it was, as ancient literary monuments testify who, after Christ's Ascension into Heaven, having travelled to Ethiopia, Persia, Hyrcania and finally to the peninsula beyond the Indus by a most difficult route attended with most serious hardships, first enlightened those nations with the light of Christian truth: and having paid to the Chief Pastor of souls the tribute of his blood, was called away to his everlasting reward in Heaven. From that time forward

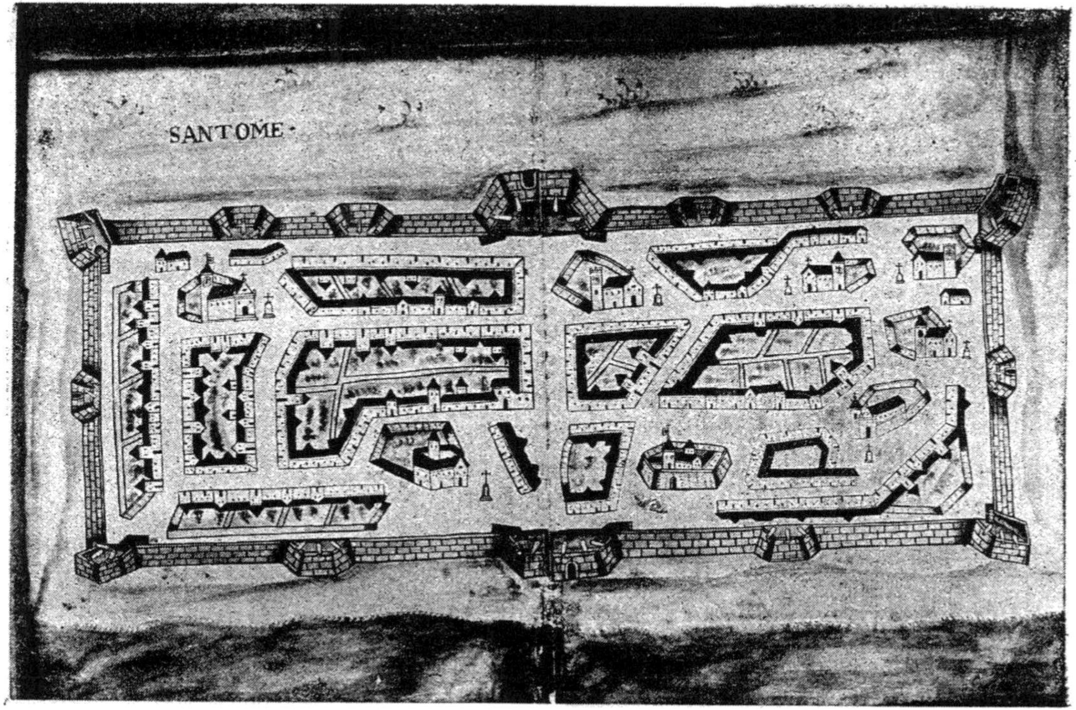

PLAN OF SAN THOMÉ ABOUT 1635—AFTER P.B. DE REZENDE.

India never altogether ceased to revere the Apostle who had deserved so well of that country. In the most ancient books of liturgical prayers, as well as in other monuments of those ancient Churches, the name and praises of Thomas were wont to be celebrated, and even in the lapse of ages after a lamentable propagation of error his memory has in no wise been defaced."

And further on in the same document where he speaks of new dioceses having been erected in India four centuries ago when the Portuguese possessions grew in extent he refers to the diocese of *Mylapore* as having been established by Paul V *in the city of St. Thomas.*

And yet, as Mgr. Zaleski, the late Delegate Apostolic of the East Indies, puts it in his work, *The Apostle St. Thomas in India* 1912, there has been a tendency even among some Catholic writers to demolish the old traditions of the Church, which play so important a part in the religious life of the people. They profess to do so in the name of what they consider historical criticism and under pretext of keeping on a level with modern scientific methods. We may add that these writers lose sight of the fact that considering the vicissitudes through which the world has passed, the absence of positive contemporary evidence in favour of these old traditions is no proof that they are not founded on fact.

PART IV.

THE LEGENDS.

I. MIRACLES.

Luis Vas de Camões (or Camoens), the most sublime figure in the history of Portuguese literature, in his great epic poem, *The Lusiads*, which celebrates the glories of Portuguese conquests in India, thus sings of St. Thomas, the Apostle, and Mylapore :—

" Here rose the potent city, Meliapor
  Named, in olden time rich, vast and grand :
Her sons their olden idols did adore
  As still adoreth that iniquitous band :
In those past ages stood she far from shore,
  When to declare glad tidings over the land
Thomé came preaching after he had trod
  A thousand regions taught to know his God.

Here came he preaching, and the while he gave
  Health to the sick, revival to the dead ;
When chance one day brought floating o'er the wave
  A forest tree of size unmeasured :
The King a Palace building lief would save
  The waif for timber, and determined
The mighty bulk of trunk ashore to train
  Bv force of engines, elephants and men.

Now was that lumber of such vasty size,
  No jot it moves, however hard they bear ;
When lo ! th' Apostle of Christ's verities
  Wastes in the business less of toil and care :
His trailing waist-cord to the tree he ties,
  Raises and *sans* an effort hales it where
A sumptuous Temple he would rear sublime,
  A fixt example for all future time.

ALTAR OF THE CHURCH ON ST. THOMAS' MOUNT.

Right well he knew how 'tis of Faith aver'd
 'Faith moveth mountains' will or nill they move,
Lending a listening ear to Holy Word:
 As Christ had taught him, so 'twas his to prove:
By such a miracle much the mob was stir'd;
 The Brahmins held it something from above;
For, seen his signs and seen his saintly life,
 They fear the loss of old prerogative.

These be the sacerdotes of Géntoo-Creed,
 That of sore jealousy felt most the pain;
They seek ill ways a thousand and take rede
 Thomé to silence or to gar him slain:
The Principal who dons the three-twine thread,
 By a deed of horror makes the lesson plain,
There be no Hatred fell, and fere and curst,
 As by false Virtue for true Virtue nurst.

One of his sons he slaughters and accuses
 Thomé of murther, who was innocent;
Bringing false witnesses, as there the use is,
 Him to the death they doom incontinent.
The Saint, assured that his best excuses
 Are his appeals to God Omnipotent,
Prepares to work before the King and Court
 A publick marvel of the major sort.

He bids be brought the body of the slain
 That it may live again and be affied
To name its slayer, and its word be tane
 As proof of testimony certified.
All saw the youth revive, arise again
 In name of Jesu Christ the Crucified;
Thomé he thanks when raised to life anew
 And names his father as the man who slew.

So much of marvel did this miracle claim,
  Straightway in Holy water bathes the King
Followed by many: These kiss Thomé's hem
  While those the praises of his Godhead sing.
Such ire the Brahmans and such furies' flame,
  Envy so pricks them with her venom'd sting,
That rousing ruffian-rout to wrath condign
  A second slaughter-plot the Priests design.

One day when preaching to the folk he stood,
  They feigned a quarrel 'mid the mob to rise:
Already Christ His Holy man endow'd
  With saintly martyrdom that open the skies.
Rained innumerable stones the crowd
  Upon the victim, sacred sacrifice,
And last a villain, hastier than the rest,
  Pierced with a cruel spear his godly breast.

Wept Ganges and Indus, true Thomé thy fate,
  Wept thee whatever lands thy foot had trod;
Yet weep thee more the souls in blissful state
  Thou led'st to don the robes of Holy Rood.
But Angels waiting at the Paradise-gate
  Meet thee with similing faces, hyming God.
We pray thee, pray that still vouchsafe thy Lord
  Unto thy Lusians His good aid afford.

(Burton's *The Lusiads*, Canto X, vs. 109-118).

ANCIENT STONE IMAGE OF ST. THOMAS AT MYLAPORE.

III. ST. THOMAS' MOUNT.

This, the traditional scene of the martyrdom of St. Thomas, is familiarly known as the "Big Mount", as Mr. J. J. Cotton has noted in his *List of Inscriptions on Tombs or Monuments in Madras;* and we should add, not "Great Mount" or "Great Mount St. Thomas" as some writers affect to call it. As far as our experience of over half a century goes St. Thomas' Mount has always been called "Big Mount" by the residents of Madras to distinguish it from the "Little Mount," which is about two miles nearer Madras. In fact it is not *big* enough to be called "Great Mount." Its proper name, *St. Thomas' Mount,* is well known to geographers and historians, and sufficiently locates and identifies the place. It is an isolated cliff of green stone and syenite 300 feet above the level of the sea and about 8 miles south-west of Madras. It is also famous for the traditional bleeding cross which was found by the Portuguese about A.D. 1547, when digging amongst the ruins of former Christian buildings for the foundation of the chapel over whose altar the cross was subsequently fixed. When discovered, spots resembling blood-stains, it is said, were observed on it which reappeared after being scraped away. There is also a painting in this church of the Mother and Child which is believed to be one of the seven portraits executed by the hand of the Apostle Luke. St. Thomas, the tradition asserts, brought it with him to India. The church itself is dedicated to "Our Lady of Expectation." Correa relates how a beacon fire was lighted nightly on the Mount for the benefit of mariners who no sooner sighted it than they struck their sails and made obeisance; and Colonel Love remarks, in this connection, in his *Vestiges of Old Madras,* 1913, that "the Native Christians of South

ANCIENT PICTURE OF THE BLESSED
VIRGIN AT ST. THOMAS' MOUNT
PAINTED ON WOOD.

INTERIOR OF CHURCH ON
ST. THOMAS' MOUNT.

ANCIENT CROSS AT ST. THOMAS' MOUNT.

India associated a hill near Madras with St. Thomas and the shrine of the Mount was venerated by people of all classes and various religions."

The cross, which is sculptured on a granite slab, has an inscription around it. There is a facsimile of it in *Epigraphica Indica*, Volume IV, page 174. "The characters," says Mr. J. J. Cotton in his work quoted above, "are Sassanian Pehlevi, 'the divine high piping Pehlevi' of Omar Khayyam's nightingale, stanza vi. It is the old heroic Sanscrit of Persia." Dr. A. C. Burnell, M.C.S., was the first in 1873 to decipher the inscription, which he attributed to the eighth century. His translation is as follows:—

"In punishment by the cross the suffering of this who is the true Christ, and God above and Guide for ever pure."

The following is a transliteration of the inscription as given by Mr. J. J. Cotton in the work just quoted, and his translation of the same:—

Mun hamich Meshikhai avakshayi madam — afras-ich Khar bukhto sur-zay mun bun dardo dena.

"He whom the suffering of the selfsame Messiah, the forgiving and upraising has saved is offering the plea whose origin was the agony of this,"

Practically the same inscription is found round the two crosses in the Valiyapalli Church at Cottayam in Travancore, followed in the case of the larger cross by a text in old Syriac from Galatians vi. 14. "But far be it from me to glory, save in the cross of our Lord Jesus Christ."

Referring to the *Pehlevi* inscription, Rev. W. H. Richards in *The Indian Christians of St. Thomas*, 1908, makes the remark that "this language owns no inscription in India later than the eighth century."

IV. THE LITTLE MOUNT.

The little Mount is a hillock about two miles away from St. Thomas' Mount and nearer Madras. It owes its name to the Portuguese, who with a view to distinguish it from the Big Mount (St. Thomas' Mount) called the former "Monte Piqueno." It contains a cave to which St. Thomas is said to have fled and sought refuge when pursued by his persecutors, and further when discovered to have escaped through a hole in it to St. Thomas' Mount where he was overtaken and speared to death. A beautiful marble altar has been erected in this cave. In 1551 the Portuguese built the present Church of our Lady of Health adjoining the cave, to which one gains access from within the Church. On the west of the Church is a Cross cut in rock before which the Apostle was wont to pray. Near by there is an opening in the rock about five to six feet in depth. It is called the well or fountain of St. Thomas, who is said to have struck the rock at this place, from which gushed forth a spring of clear water, which quenched the thirst of the multitude hearing him preach, and which is believed to have possessed also healing qualities.

THE LITTLE MOUNT CHURCH.

MARBLE ALTAR OF ST. THOMAS IN THE CAVE
AT THE LITTLE MOUNT.

V. CONCLUDING REMARKS.

Some interesting details in connection with these legends, as related by old Portuguese and other writers, will be found in Col. Love's *Vestiges of Old Madras.* Even if they are pure inventions, it must be observed that this fact does not in any way militate against our chief contention that the Apostle did come to Southern India and was martyred on a hill near Madras, seeing that it is supported, as we have shown, by quite other independent evidence. On the other hand, the absence of positive evidence in support of these legends is no proof that the main facts, however much they may have been added to and distorted, are not based on reality, or are by any means out of keeping with the belief founded on scripture that the Apostles went forth into the world endowed with the gift of speech and the power of performing miracles.

It may here be mentioned that the Rev. Fr. H. Hosten, S. J., of Darjeeling, who spent some time at San Thomé about the beginning of 1921, devoted his stay here to investigations connected with the story of St. Thomas and of his traditional connection with San Thomé, Mylapore, taking notes archæological, historical and bibliographical. He has since started publishing weekly in the *Catholic Herald of India,* beginning with the issue of 27th July 1921, tentative articles on his findings, which are eliciting corrections and additions, especially from the St. Thomas Christians of Malabar, and have led further to measures being taken to have translated into English a volume on St. Thomas and the Malabar traditions by the Rev. Fr. Bernard of St. Thomas, T. O. C. D. This work was published in

Malayalam in 1917, and filling about 500 pages would, Fr. Hosten remarks, be of the greatest service to scholars, as the whole question of early Christianity in Malabar is there reviewed in the light of archæology, native records and tradition.

FEAST OF ST. THOMAS,
21st December 1921.

MIRACULOUS SPRING AT THE LITTLE MOUNT.

AUTHORITIES CONSULTED.

The following are the principal authorities consulted and referred to in the text:—

The Bible.

The Roman Breviary.

The Roman Martyrolyy.

Paul V, *The Papal Bull* of 1606, erecting the Diocese of San Thomë de Meliapor.

Leo XIII, *Apostolic Letter* of 1886, establishing the Hierarchy in India.

Ancient Syriac Documents, London, 1864.

Dr. Burkit in *Encyclopædia Britannica*, Vol. XXVI, 11th Edn.

Rev. H. Thurston in *Catholic Encyclopedia*, Vol., XIV, p. 658.

Rev. James Doyle in *Catholic Encyclopedia*, Vol. XIII, p. 382.

W. R. Philipps in *Indian Antiquary*, 1903, page 1 ff, page 145 ff, and 1904 p. 31.

J. F. Fleet in *Journal of the Royal Asiatic Society*, London, April 1905.

J. Kennedy in *Journal of the Royal Asiatic Society*, London, October 1906, and in *The East and the West*, April 1907.

Milne Rae, *The Syrian Church in India*, Edinburg, 1892.

Medlycott, *India and the Apostle Thomas*, London, 1905.

Richards, *Indian Christians of St. Thomas*, London, 1908.

Mgr. Zaleski, *The Apostle Thomas in India*, 1912.

Vincent A. Smith, *The Early History of India*, 1914.

" " " *The Oxford History of India*, 1919.

The Travancore State Manual, 1906.

Hunter, *Imperial Gazetteer of India*, 1886.

J. J. Cotton, *List of Inscriptions on Tombs or Monuments in Madras*, 1905.

Sewell, *Dynasties of Southern India*, 1883.

Macleane, *Manual of the Administration of the Madras Presidency*, Glossary, Vol. iii, 1893.

Yule and Burnell, *Hobson Jobson*, 1903.

The Cochin Census Report, 1901, as quoted by Thurston in *Castes and Tribes of Southern India*, 1909.

Col. Love, *Vestiges of Old Madras*, 1913.

Camoens, *The Lusiads* translated by Burton, London, 1880.

Lightning Source UK Ltd.
Milton Keynes UK
UKHW021355110119
335397UK00005B/187/P

9 781372 619670